DELIA SMITH'S CHRISTMAS

DELIA SMITH'S CHRISTMAS

BBC Books

For my Mother –
thanks for all the lovely Christmases.

ABOUT THE AUTHOR

Delia Smith is a best-selling cookery author whose cookery books have sold over 5 million copies. She has become the Mrs Beeton of our times. Her other books include *Delia Smith's Complete Illustrated Cookery Course*, *One is Fun*, *Frugal Food*, *Delia Smith's Summer Collection*, and *Journey into God*. She is married to the writer and editor Michael Wynn Jones and they live in Suffolk.

With very special thanks to Mary Cox and Caroline Liddell for their help with the recipe testing, and also to Suzanne Webber, Nicky Copeland and Christine Medcalf for all their patient editorial advice and help.

Published by BBC Books,
a division of BBC Enterprises Limited,
Woodlands, 80 Wood Lane, London W12 0TT

First published in hardback 1990
Published in paperback 1994
© Delia Smith 1990
The moral right of the author has been asserted.

ISBN 0 563 37064 5 (paperback)

0 563 36048 8 (hardback)

Designed by Elaine Partington
Illustrations by Angela McAllister
Illustrations on pp. 76–7 by Kate Simunek
Food photography by James Murphy
Location photography by David Steen
Front cover photograph by Norman Holland
Props by Andrea Lambton
Food prepared by Catherine Calland

Set in Baskerville by Ace Filmsetting Ltd, Frome
Printed and bound in Great Britain by Butler and Tanner Ltd, Frome
Colour separations by Technik Ltd, Berkhamsted
Jacket printed by Belmont Press Ltd, Northampton

Page 2: A festive wreath decorating Crabtree & Evelyn's shop in Oxford.

Contents

Introduction

If there's one person in the world who probably needs this book more than anyone else, it's me. For years my own Christmas preparations have been, to say the least, fragmented and fraught: recipes here, notes there, and fading memories of what I might have done last year if only I could be sure! What I needed, it seemed to me, was a sort of personal Christmas organiser, something I could reach for in October and keep by me as a guide all the way through to the point where the last of the Christmas leftovers have been dealt with.

Then I began to think: if that's what *I* need, how many other people might need the same? It would be nice of course to be able to say at this point that the contents of this book can zip you through all that Christmas catering without a worry or a care. Unfortunately that is not the case, because unless you are superhuman, believe me, there will still be some hectic days ahead of you. But what I have set out to do here is to be a sort of friend in the background, providing practical information, offering new and different recipes (as well as the more traditional ones), and if not entirely removing the pressure of Christmas cooking then going some way to ensuring its success.

Christmas has its critics and, if we were honest, I'm sure each one of us has, at some time, wished we could quietly quit the planet and come back when it was over. On the other hand, at what other time of the year can we turn our minds to the sheer joy of feasting? The sharing of fine food and wines with family and friends is a deeply ingrained human (as well as religious) activity, without which our lives would surely be diminished.

As a veteran of many a Christmas campaign, my final message to you is not to worry. You will be pressured, you will get grumpy, but it *will* all be worth it. Just set your mind on that glorious moment on Christmas Day when the last of the washing-up has been done. By then you will probably have enough food in the house to last for several days, so fill your glass, put your feet up and forget all about it for another year!

Delia Smith

The Christmas window at Charbonnel et Walker's shop in London.

Lists and More Lists!

There is a Christmas equation that goes something like this: the shorter the shopping time to Christmas, the longer the queues; the longer the queues, the shorter the memory. On more than one occasion I have discovered I am missing some vital ingredient at 3.00 pm on Christmas Eve – and that is not the best time to dash off to the supermarket.

So, for my benefit as much as yours, here follow some shopping lists based on the recipes and suggestions in this book. If, at some time well ahead of the Christmas rush, you can take a few moments to study them, make your own list of what you're going to need. Then perhaps start to collect a few items week by week and you might be spared some of the last-minute jostling, shoving and panic buying.

General Food Shopping

Sugar – caster
  icing
  granulated
Flour – self-raising
  plain
  wholewheat
  strong
Almonds – ground
  whole
  flaked
Pecan nuts
Brazil nuts
No-soak apricots
Currants, raisins, sultanas
Candied peels
Muscatels
Dates
Prunes
Glacé fruits and glacé
  cherries
Cloves

Juniper
Cinnamon
Mixed spice
Mace
Coriander seeds
Nutmegs
Ginger – fresh root
  candied
Creamed coconut
Luxury plain dessert
  chocolate
Chestnut purée
Marrons glacés
Glycerine
Liquid glucose
Gelatine
Suet
Yeast
Filo pastry
Oil – olive
  groundnut

Wine vinegar – red
  white
Dried porcini mushrooms
  – available at Italian
  delicatessens and
  specialised food shops
Oranges
Lemons
Bramley apples
Eggs
Butter
Rum
Port
Brandy
Madeira
Barley wine
Stout
Sherry
Mixer drinks

General Non-food Shopping

Turkey-width foil
Cling film
Christmas crackers
Napkins
Party streamers
Cake boards
Greaseproof paper
Silicone paper
Paper sweet cases
Preserving jars
Small metal pudding
    basins or ramekins
Fluted quiche tin

Lattice cutter
Extra mince pie tins
Hangover remedy
Roasting tin for turkey
    (check size)
Pudding basin
Holly-leaf cutter, silver
    balls
Kitchen paper
Muslin
Swiss-roll tin 8 × 12 ins
    (20 × 30 cm)

Cake tins – 7 inch (18 cm)
    square, 8 inch (20 cm)
    round and boards
Decorative candles
Tree lights in working
    order
Spare lightbulbs
Wrapping paper, gift tags
String and Selotape
Cocktail sticks
Spare fuses and fusewire
Batteries

Week Before Christmas/Groceries

Tea, coffee
Butter
Extra milk
Cheese, cheese biscuits
Bread and rolls
Frozen pastry
Bacon, sausages,
    sausagemeat
Fresh cream – single
    double

Eggs
Redcurrant jelly
Cranberries
Parmesan cheese
Trifle sponges
Salt, black peppercorns
Rice
Marmalade
Yoghurt, fromage frais
Dried fruit

Capers, gherkins
Pickled walnuts
Fresh orange juice
NOTE: Now is the time to
decide which turkey
stuffing you intend to use
and buy the appropriate
ingredients (see pages
192–3).

Last-minute Fruit and Vegetables

General guideline: 4 oz (110 g) vegetables per person per meal

Potatoes – roasting
    salad
Parsnips
Carrots
Brussels sprouts
Red cabbage
Mushrooms – flat
    oyster

Onions
Spring onions
Watercress
Celery
Parsley
Chestnuts (for roasting)
Garlic

Bramley apples
Oranges
Lemons
Grapes
Pineapple
Grapefruit
Bananas

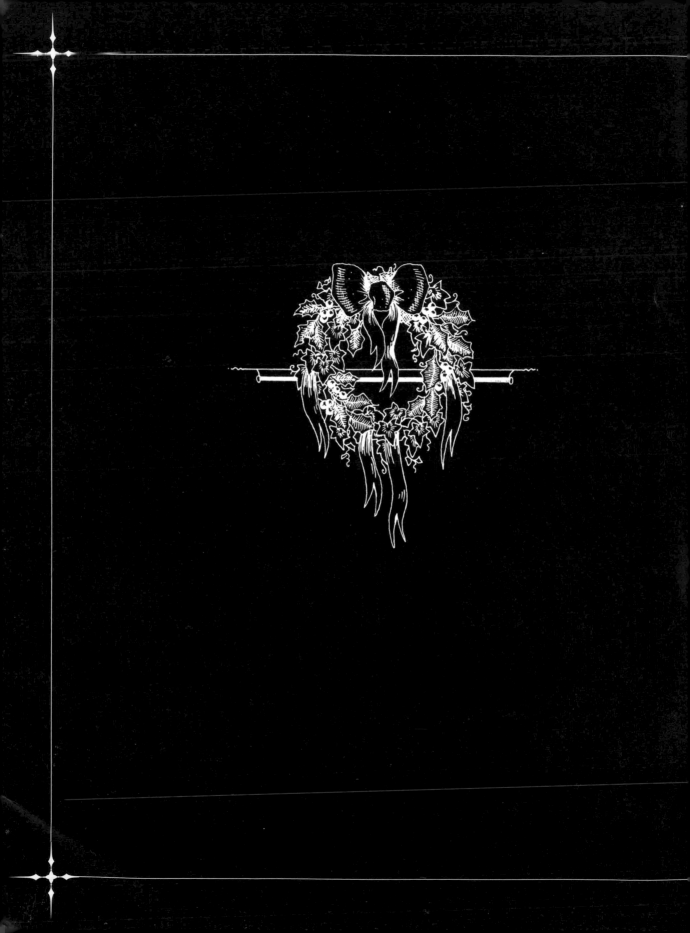

CHAPTER 1

All Kinds
OF
Christmas
Cakes

One of the first, and probably most pleasurable, of the advance preparations for Christmas is making the cake. For me, it's all the more enjoyable because I haven't yet got caught in the build-up of panic and pressure that will be inevitable later on. I am still under the happy illusion that this year is going to be well-planned and ordered – after all, here am I making the cake weeks ahead!

Ideally, and if everything is going to plan, we are at the end of October or the beginning of November. Cakes made now, and 'fed' regularly in the meantime (see page 13), will have matured and be at their very best for Christmas. The first mouthful may be a long way off yet, but making the cake will provide the first evocative preview as all the fruits and spices, citrus peels and booze combine to fill the house with that unmistakable Christmassy baking aroma. The joy of anticipation starts right here.

If you haven't made a Christmas cake before, the first step is to choose which kind of cake you want: the dark, spicy, moist, traditional variety, or perhaps one of the lighter versions? Maybe you've been making the same kind for several years, and you'd like to try something new? In the following pages you will find a cake for every taste but, first, a few notes on Christmas cakes you may find helpful.

Ingredients

Dried fruit: I happen to live among keen Christmas cake enthusiasts and at this time each autumn word gets round that so-and-so has the most beautiful plump sultanas and the best currants this year are at such-and-such a shop. Well, not everyone has the time for that sort of detail but it *is* worth noting that dried fruits do vary in quality. It is important not only to buy the new season's crop, but also to look out for the moistest, plumpest fruits: if you always buy the ones in cellophane packets you can *see* the quality. And remember that very often the best dried fruit comes from good supermarkets because they have a large turnover and their stock hasn't been sitting on a shelf for weeks.

Candied peel: If you want to give your cake that five-star flavour, then go for *whole* candied peel and, again, look for the bright, glistening signs of the new season's crop. No matter how good the original quality of the ready-chopped peel, it invariably seems to lose something in the chopping. Cutting it yourself is extra work, I know, but if you have a really sharp knife (or kitchen scissors) and something good on the radio it really is worth the effort.

Alcohol or no alcohol? Personally I think it is the obvious affinity between the dried fruits of the vine and their fermented and distilled juices, and their combining in the cooking, that gives that distinctive seasonal flavour to the cakes. However, I get a number of letters from people who never touch alcohol, so let me say that in the following recipes freshly squeezed orange juice can be substituted for the booze – except in the case of the Creole Christmas cake (see page 18), where the combined flavours of the different spirits and liqueurs are the whole point of the cake.

Timings

Baking: It is here that a cookery writer steps into a minefield. First of all conventional ovens do vary and it is worth having them tested every now and again. Second, it is quite possible to make exactly the same cake (and I have had this confirmed by someone who makes at least a dozen each year for presents) and to find each one cooking in a slightly different time. On top of that there are fan-assisted ovens which are a law unto themselves! To the beginner I can only say that no timing for a rich fruit cake can be absolutely precise, and be prepared for a Christmas cake to vary even up to an hour either way. So . . .

Is it or isn't it cooked? The best test is your own sense of touch. If you press the centre of the cake gently with your little finger and it feels springy and firm, without leaving an impression on the surface, then the cake is cooked.

Curdling: It can sometimes happen that, when you are creaming the mixture for the cake, the beaten eggs are added to the sugar-and-fat mixture too quickly, causing the whole mixture to separate. This breaking-up means that some of the air incorporated at the creaming stage will escape and the finished cake will be slightly heavier. For beginners, the way to avoid this is to add the beaten eggs just a teaspoonful at a time, whisking preferably with a hand whisk. If it does curdle, though, don't worry: the cake won't be as light, but it's not a disaster.

Storing and feeding the cake: I like to wrap the cake in a double layer of greaseproof paper and then in double foil. Secure it all with an elastic band, then keep it in a polythene container till needed. For those who like a well-brandied cake, a little 'feeding' of the cake at odd intervals (say, weekly) before Christmas will add an extra dimension to it. This is done by making small holes in the top and bottom of the cake with a darning needle, then spooning over teaspoonfuls of brandy to soak in through the holes and permeate the cake.

THE CLASSIC CHRISTMAS CAKE

·

*T*his, with no apologies, is a Christmas cake that has been in print for 21 years, has been made and loved by thousands and is, along with the Traditional Christmas pudding (see page 37), one of the most popular recipes I've produced. It's rich, dark and quite moist, so will not suit those who like a crumblier texture. Recently we took some of these cakes along to book-signing sessions up and down the country and were quite amazed to see so many people take a mouthful and then buy a book!

1 lb (450 g) currants	2 oz (50 g) almonds, chopped ✓
6 oz (175 g) sultanas	(the skins can be left on)
6 oz (175 g) raisins	1 dessertspoon black treacle
2 oz (50 g) glacé cherries, rinsed, dried and finely chopped	The grated zest of 1 lemon ✓
	The grated zest of 1 orange ✓
2 oz (50 g) mixed candied peel, finely chopped	4 oz (110 g) whole blanched almonds (only if you don't intend to ice the cake)
3 tablespoons brandy	
8 oz (225 g) plain flour ✓	You will need an 8 inch (20 cm) round cake tin or a 7 inch (18 cm) square tin, greased and lined with greaseproof paper (see page 19). Tie a band of brown paper round the outside of the tin for extra protection.
½ teaspoon salt ✓	
¼ teaspoon freshly grated nutmeg ✓	
½ teaspoon ground mixed spice ✓	
8 oz (225 g) unsalted butter ✓	
8 oz (225 g) soft brown sugar ✓	
4 eggs, size 1	

You need to begin this cake the night before you want to bake it. All you do is weigh out the dried fruit and mixed peel, place it in a mixing bowl and mix in the brandy as evenly and thoroughly as possible. Cover the bowl with a clean tea-cloth and leave the fruit aside to absorb the brandy for 12 hours.

Next day pre-heat the oven to gas mark 1, 275°F (140°C). Then measure out all the rest of the ingredients, ticking them off to make quite sure they're all there. The treacle will be easier to measure if you remove the lid and place the tin in a small pan of barely simmering water.

Now begin the cake by sifting the flour, salt and spices into a large mixing bowl, lifting the sieve up high to give the flour a good airing. Next, in a separate large mixing bowl, whisk the butter and sugar together until it's light, pale and fluffy. Now beat the eggs in a separate bowl and add them to the creamed mixture a tablespoonful at a time; keep the whisk running until all the egg is incorporated. If you add the eggs slowly by degrees like this the mixture won't curdle (see page 13). If it does, don't worry, any cake full of such beautiful things can't fail to taste good! When all the egg has been added fold in the flour and spices, using gentle, folding movements and not beating at all (this is to keep all that precious air in). Now fold in the fruit, peel, chopped nuts and treacle and finally the grated lemon and orange zests.

Next, using a large kitchen spoon, transfer the cake mixture into the prepared tin, spread it out evenly with the back of a spoon and, if you don't intend to ice the cake, lightly drop the whole blanched almonds in circles or squares all over the surface. Finally cover the top of the cake with a double square of greaseproof paper with a 50p-size hole in the centre (this gives extra protection during the long slow cooking). Bake the cake on the lowest shelf of the oven for 4½–4¾ hours. Sometimes it can take up to ½–¾ hour longer than this, but in any case don't look till at least 4 hours have passed.

Cool the cake for 30 minutes in the tin, then remove it to a wire rack to finish cooling. When it's cold 'feed' it (see page 13), wrap it in double greaseproof paper secured with an elastic band and either wrap again in foil or store in an airtight tin. You can now feed it at odd intervals until you need to ice or eat it.

SCOTTISH WHISKY DUNDEE CAKE

·

*W*hen *people tell me they don't like rich, very moist fruit cakes at Christmas I always recommend a Dundee cake. It has a lighter and much more crumbly texture than the Classic Christmas cake (see page 14) and the addition of some Scotch malt whisky gives it a special Christmas edge.*

6 oz (175 g) currants	Milk, if necessary
6 oz (175 g) sultanas	2 level tablespoons ground almonds
4 oz (110 g) glacé cherries, rinsed, dried and cut into halves	The grated rind of 1 small orange
	The grated rind of 1 small lemon
3 oz (75 g) mixed candied peel, finely chopped	4 oz (110 g) whole blanched almonds (only if you don't intend to ice the cake)
3 tablespoons whisky	1 miniature bottle (3½ tablespoons) of
5 oz (150 g) butter, at room temperature	single malt Scotch whisky (for 'feeding')
5 oz (150 g) soft brown sugar	
3 eggs, size 1	You will need a 7 inch (18 cm) square or
8 oz (225 g) plain flour	8 inch (20 cm) round cake tin, greased and
1 teaspoon baking powder	lined with greaseproof paper (see page 19).

Begin the night before by weighing the fruit and peel into a bowl and sprinkling it with the 3 tablespoons of whisky. Mix well, cover and leave overnight.

Pre-heat the oven to gas mark 3, 325°F (170°C). Put the butter and sugar in a mixing bowl and beat with a wooden spoon until light and fluffy – or use an electric mixer for more speed. Whisk the eggs separately then, a little at a time, beat them into the creamed butter and sugar. Next, using a large tablespoon, carefully *fold* in the sifted flour and baking powder. Your mixture needs to be of a soft, dropping consistency so, if it seems too dry, add a dessertspoon of milk.

Now, carefully fold in the ground almonds and then the currants, sultanas, cherries, mixed peel and orange and lemon rinds. Then spoon the mixture into the prepared cake tin, smoothing it out evenly with the back of the spoon. If you don't intend to ice the cake, arrange the whole blanched almonds in circles on top of the mixture, but do this carefully and lightly; if they are pressed in they will sink during the baking. Place the cake in the centre of the oven and bake for 2–2½ hours or until the centre is firm and springy to the touch.

Let the cake cool in the tin for 30 minutes before taking it out to finish cooling on a wire rack. Then 'feed' it (see page 13), wrap it in double greaseproof paper and store it in foil or an airtight tin till needed. If you like you can feed it again before icing or eating.

LIGHT GLACÉ FRUIT CAKE

·

This is an absolutely delightful alternative Christmas cake; one for connoisseurs, I think. It's light in colour with a fragrant flavour and the glacé fruits look jewel-like when you cut it open. It works well with marzipan and icing or a glacé fruit and nut topping.

8 oz (225 g) sultanas	The grated zest of 1 medium lemon
4 oz (110 g) dried apricots, roughly chopped	8 oz (225 g) unsalted butter, at room temperature
3 tablespoons brandy	8 oz (225 g) caster sugar
4 oz (110 g) pecan nuts, roughly chopped	4 eggs, size 2
4 oz (110 g) glacé pineapple, roughly chopped	2 oz (50 g) ground almonds
	8 oz (225 g) plain flour, sifted
6 oz (175 g) red, green and yellow glacé cherries, roughly chopped	¼ teaspoon salt
4 oz (110 g) whole, mixed candied peel, chopped small	You will need an 8 inch (20 cm) round cake tin or a 7 inch (18 cm) square tin, greased and lined with a double thickness of greaseproof paper (see page 19). Tie a band of brown paper round the outside of the tin for extra protection.
2 oz (50 g) angelica, chopped small	
2 oz (50 g) crystallised ginger, chopped small	
The grated zest of 1 medium orange	

Begin the night before by placing the sultanas and chopped apricots in a large mixing bowl. Stir in the brandy, cover and leave overnight.

Pre-heat the oven to gas mark 3, 325°F (170°C). Add the rest of the nuts, fruit and peels into the sultanas and apricots. Tick everything off as you go.

Now whisk with an electric hand whisk the butter and sugar in another large mixing bowl until pale and fluffy. Then beat the eggs and add them to the butter and sugar, a very small amount at a time, whisking well after every addition. When all the eggs are incorporated, lightly fold in the sifted flour and salt, followed by the ground almonds and then all the fruit, nuts, etc. Now transfer the mixture to the tin, levelling it off with the back of a spoon, and place the tin in the oven so the top of it is more or less in the centre. Bake the cake for 1 hour then place a double sheet of greaseproof paper over the top of the tin and turn the heat down to gas mark 2, 300°F (150°C), for a further 2–2¼ hours. When it's cooked it will have begun to shrink away from the sides of the tin and be springy in the centre when you press lightly with your little finger. You can leave this cake in the tin till it's absolutely cold then peel off the papers and wrap it in double greaseproof paper before storing in an airtight tin.

CREOLE CHRISTMAS CAKE

·

*T*his recipe is for those who want a complete break with tradition and to try something completely new. On a visit to Trinidad, the wife of the chairman of Billington's, who import the dark raw sugar of the West Indies, tasted a most delectable cake and was so struck by it that she managed to acquire the recipe from the wife of the local sugar plantation manager. Here I offer my own adaptation and would describe it as being much more fruit than cake; it's extremely moist, so much so that it could be eaten as a dessert with whipped cream. Don't be put off by the large amount of alcohol or the length of time the fruit is steeped in it, the wonderful flavour of the cake makes every drop totally worthwhile.

FOR THE PRE-SOAKING:

3 tablespons rum
3 tablespoons brandy
3 tablespoons cherry brandy
3 tablespoons port
3 tablespoons water
1½ teaspoons Angostura bitters
½ teaspoon ground cinnamon
½ teaspoon ground nutmeg
½ teaspoon ground cloves
½ teaspoon salt
1½ teaspoons vanilla extract
1 tablespoon molasses sugar
1 lb (450 g) raisins
8 oz (225 g) currants

4 oz (110 g) stoned no-soak prunes, chopped
2 oz (50 g) glacé cherries, chopped
4 oz (110 g) mixed candied peel
2 oz (50 g) mixed chopped nuts

FOR THE CAKE:

9 oz (250 g) self-raising flour
9 oz (250 g) demerara sugar
9 oz (250 g) butter, at room temperature
5 eggs, size 1

You will need an 8 inch (20 cm) square cake tin, greased, and the base and sides lined with a double thickness of greaseproof paper (see opposite).

One week before you intend to bake the cake, measure out the rum, brandy, cherry brandy, port, water and bitters into a large saucepan. Then add the rest of the pre-soaking ingredients, ticking them with a pencil as you go to make sure nothing gets left out. Now stir and bring the mixture up to simmering point, then, keeping the heat low, simmer very gently for 15 minutes. After that allow everything to cool completely then pour the mixture into a large jar with a lid or an airtight plastic container and leave it in the refrigerator for 7 days, shaking or stirring it around from time to time.

When you're ready to bake the cake, pre-heat the oven to gas mark 1, 275°F (140°C). All you do is measure out the flour, sugar and softened butter into a very large mixing bowl then add the eggs and either whisk or beat with a wooden spoon until everything is evenly blended. Now gradually fold in the fruit mixture until it's all evenly distributed. Then spoon the mixture into the prepared tin, levelling the surface with the back of the spoon. Bake the cake in the centre of the oven for 3 hours without opening the door, then cover the cake with a double thickness of greaseproof paper and continue to bake it for a further hour or until the centre feels springy when lightly touched.

Cool the cake for 45 minutes in the tin, then remove it to a wire rack to finish cooling. When it's completely cold, wrap in double greaseproof paper and then foil and store in an airtight tin or polythene box. There's no need to feed this cake as it already has enough booze, but it does improve with keeping for about 1 month before cutting.

NOTE: This is too rich a cake to marzipan and ice so either leave it as it is or I think it's splendid topped with the Glazed nut topping (see page 31). Then it should be stored without wrapping in a polythene box.

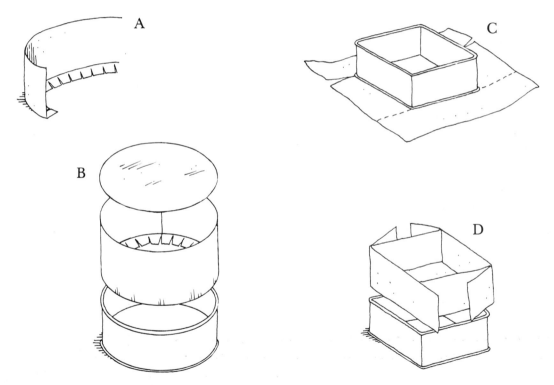

LINING CAKE TINS

For a round tin: cut a strip of paper slightly longer than the circumference of the tin. Fold back 1 inch (2.5 cm) along its length and snip this at intervals, cutting at a slight angle to the fold (A). Grease the tin, then press the paper around the sides. Finally, cut a circle of paper – using the tin as a template – to fit in the base (B).
For a square tin: cut a piece of paper to size by measuring the length and width of the tin and adding twice its depth. Centre the tin on the paper, then make four cuts from the paper's edge to the corners of the tin (C). Grease the tin and fit the paper inside, folding and overlapping at the corners (D).

STOLLEN

·

*A*t Christmas time in Austria they traditionally serve something called stollen (see page 22): it is a rich, fruity yeast bread filled with marzipan and topping with a light glacé icing. If you have a number of people staying over the holiday this is wonderful served warmed through at breakfast. If it is not all eaten when it's fresh you can also lightly toast it in slices. In fact it is so good it is worth making two and freezing one (it freezes beautifully).

5 fl oz (150 ml) milk	1½ oz (40 g) no-soak apricots, chopped
2 oz (50 g) caster sugar	1 oz (25 g) glacé cherries, rinsed, dried
2 level teaspoons dried yeast	and quartered
12 oz (350 g) strong white bread flour	1 oz (25 g) almonds, chopped
¼ teaspoon salt	The grated zest of ½ lemon
4 oz (110 g) softened butter	6 oz (175 g) marzipan
1 egg, size 2, beaten	
1½ oz (40 g) currants	FOR THE GLAZE:
2 oz (50 g) sultanas	4 oz (110 g) icing sugar, sifted
1 oz (25 g) mixed candied peel, finely diced	1 tablespoon lemon juice

PRE-HEAT THE OVEN TO GAS MARK 5, 375°F (190°C)

Warm the milk, first of all, till you can just still dip your little finger in it. Then pour it into a glass jug, add 1 teaspoon of the sugar along with the dried yeast and leave it until it forms a frothy head of about 1 inch (2.5 cm). Meanwhile sift 11 oz (300 g) of the flour together with the salt and remaining sugar into a mixing bowl, and make a well in the centre. Pour the milk and yeast mixture into this, then add the softened butter and beaten egg. Mix everything together – either with your hands or with a wooden spoon – until the mixture is well blended and leaves the side of the bowl cleanly. Then work in the fruits, peel, nuts and lemon zest, distributing them as evenly as possible. Knead the dough on a working surface for 5 minutes until it is springy and elastic.

Now leave the dough in a warm place, covered with cling film, until it has doubled in size (the time this takes can vary depending on the temperature – it could take up to 2 hours). After that turn the risen dough out on to a board floured with the reserved 1 oz (25 g) of flour, and knock the air out of it and knead the dough until it is smooth and elastic. At this stage roll or press out the dough to an oblong 10 × 8 inches (25 × 20 cm). Using your hands, roll out the marzipan to form a sausage-shape and place this along the centre of the dough, finishing just short of the edges.

Fold the dough over the marzipan and carefully place the whole thing on a baking sheet, allowing plenty of room for expansion. Leave it to prove in a warm place until it has doubled in size again, then bake in the oven for 35–40 minutes. Allow it to cool on the baking sheet for about 5 minutes before lifting it on to a wire rack to finish cooling.

Meanwhile make the glaze by mixing the sifted icing sugar with the lemon juice, then use a small palette knife to spread this all over the top surface of the stollen (while it is still warm). Serve as fresh as possible, cut into thick slices, with or without butter.

LAST-MINUTE CHRISTMAS MINCEMEAT CAKE

·

*T*his is a wonderful cake for the really harassed who meant either to make or buy a cake and never got round to it. It is unbelievably quick and easy yet has a marvellous flavour and a good moist texture.

1 lb (450 g) good quality mincemeat	The grated zest of 1 small lemon
8 oz (225 g) wholemeal flour	3 eggs, size 1 or 2
3 level teaspoons baking powder	4 oz (110 g) whole blanched almonds
5 oz (150 g) dark brown sugar	(only if you don't intend to ice the cake)
5 oz (150 g) softened butter or soft margarine	
6 oz (175 g) mixed dried fruit	You will need an 8 inch (20 cm) round
2 oz (50 g) walnuts, chopped	cake tin, greased, and the base and sides
The grated zest of 1 small orange	lined with greaseproof paper
	(see page 19).

PRE-HEAT THE OVEN TO GAS MARK 3, 325°F (170°C)

First place all the ingredients (except the almonds) in a large mixing bowl. There is no need to beat the eggs, just break them in; but it is a good idea to sift the flour to give it an airing, then you can tip in the bits of bran left in the sieve afterwards.

Now, if you have an electric hand whisk, just switch on and beat everything together thoroughly. If not, a wooden spoon will do, but it takes a bit longer. Next, spoon the mixture evenly into the tin, level off the surface and, if you're using them, arrange the almonds in circles over the top.

Bake the cake for about 1 hour 30 minutes, or until the centre springs back when lightly touched. Then let it cool in the tin for 30 minutes before turning it out to finish cooling on a wire rack. If you want to and you have time you can 'feed' if with brandy (see page 13), but it tastes wonderful anyway.

NOTE: It is important to use a good quality mincemeat if you are not using the homemade recipe. In some of the cheaper brands there is too much liquid for this type of cake.

The cooking time for the cake varies from oven to oven, sometimes taking up to 2 hours. The only way to test it is to gently press the centre of the cake with your finger. If it is firm and springy, and no impression is left, then it is ready.

Stollen (see page 20).

CHRISTMAS CAKE ICINGS AND TOPPINGS

It has long been my conviction that Christmas is not the best time for creative cake decorations. I do realise that there are those whose lives are more organised than mine, who have Christmas all sewn up early and who can look forward to a leisurely period devoted to wielding a piping-bag and modelling paste. To those enviable people I can only recommend an inspiring book, *The Icing on the Cake*, by Greg Robinson and Max Schofield (Bloomsbury).

But for the rest of us pressured Christmas caterers I have devised the simplest, speediest Christmas cake decorations possible. Bearing in mind that in whatever shape the icing sugar and marzipan arrive on the cake they will always taste the same, the key to these suggestions of mine is that they will look classy with a minimum of effort. One important point: it is now possible to buy good quality fondant and almond icing ready-made.

◆ ◆ ◆

ROYAL ICING

FOR A ROUGH 'SNOW' SCENE FOR A 7 INCH (18 CM) SQUARE
OR AN 8 INCH (20 CM) ROUND CAKE

I confess this has often been for me a last-minute affair late on Christmas Eve. Very often there's the odd robin or Father Christmas handed down through generations to decorate with, but failing that a sprig of holly in the centre of the cake will give a festive touch.

1 lb 2 oz (500 g) icing sugar, sifted	1 teaspoon glycerine
3 egg whites, size 2	

Place the egg whites in a bowl, then stir in the icing sugar, a spoonful at a time, until the icing falls thickly from the spoon. At this stage, stop adding any more sugar and whisk with an electric whisk for 10 minutes or until the icing stands up in stiff peaks, then stir in the glycerine.

Now spread the icing all over the base and sides of the cake as evenly as possible using a palette knife. Switch to a broad-bladed knife (or smaller palette knife) to 'spike' the icing all over to give a snow-scene effect. Leave the cake overnight for the icing to dry out before placing it in a container till needed.

ALMOND ICING

·

FOR A 7 INCH (18 CM) SQUARE OR AN 8 INCH (20 CM) ROUND CAKE

Ideally, before you cover it with Royal icing, almond icing should be left for several days after it has been applied to the cake, to dry out its oiliness. But if you find you don't have the time for that, then I suggest you top it with the rough 'snow' icing (see page 24), which is thick enough for the almond oil not to discolour it.

12 oz (350 g) ground almonds	⅓ teaspoon pure almond extract
6 oz (175 g) icing sugar plus extra for dusting	1 teaspoon lemon juice
	1 teaspoon brandy
6 oz (175 g) caster sugar	3 eggs, size 2, 1 of them separated

Begin by sifting the icing and caster sugar into a large bowl, then stir in the whole eggs and the egg yolk. Place the bowl over a pan of barely simmering water and whisk for about 12 minutes until the mixture is thick and fluffy. Then remove the bowl from the heat and sit the base in a couple of inches of cold water. Whisk in the almond extract, lemon juice and brandy and continue to whisk until the mixture is cool. At this point stir in the ground almonds and knead to form a firm paste.

Now divide the paste by cutting off one-third of it. Dust a working surface with icing sugar and roll the smaller piece of paste into an 8 inch (20 cm) square (you can either use a ruler for this or else the base of the cake tin as a guide). Next brush the top of the cake all over with egg white, then turn it upside down and place it centrally on the rolled-out almond paste. Using a palette knife, press the edges of the paste up all round the edges of the cake, then turn the cake the right way up to deal with the sides.

Once again dust the working surface with icing sugar, and roll out the rest of the paste into a length 14 × 6 inches (35 × 15 cm). Divide this in half lengthways, then brush the sides of the cake with egg white and fix the two strips of almond paste all around the sides – you can smooth over the joins, first with a knife then with a rolling pin. Now leave the cake, covered with a clean cloth, for as long as possible up to 7 days.

NOTE: If you wish to use ready-made almond icing (marzipan) you will need a 1½ lb (700 g) quantity to cover a 7 inch (18 cm) square cake as above.

◆━●━◆

DECORATED HOLLY LEAF CAKE

·

FOR THE FONDANT ICING FOR A 7 INCH (18 CM) SQUARE
OR AN 8 INCH (20 CM) ROUND CAKE

This is a simple but tasteful design for those who want to go a step further than the quick snow scene. To get royal icing really flat and smooth has always demanded a great deal of skill, but now that fondant icing has become more popular everything has been simplified down to simply rolling out the icing and fitting it on to the cake. Holly leaf cutters are available at good kitchen shops, shops which specialise in cake decoration or by mail order from the address on page 219.

1¼ lb (560 g) icing sugar plus extra for dusting
2 egg whites, size 1
3 level tablespoons liquid glucose (available from chemists)
63 silver balls to decorate

You will also need a 10 inch (25 cm) round cake board or an 11 inch (28 cm) square board and a holly leaf cutter 1⅛ inch (2.8 cm) in length.

First sift the icing sugar into a large bowl, then add 1½ egg whites, which is just under 2 fl oz (55 ml), and reserve the rest of the egg white for later. Add the liquid glucose. Now start to mix everything with a wooden spoon and then finish off with your hands. As soon as you have a ball of icing, transfer it to a surface dusted with icing sugar and start to knead it in the same way as you would knead bread dough. (I'm afraid it will take 10 minutes or so, so you may need some good music on – or else use it as an opportunity to get rid of all your hidden aggressions!)

If the dough becomes a bit sticky just add a little more sifted icing sugar. When the 10 minutes are up, leave the icing on one side covered with a cloth for 30 minutes.

To ice the cake, first reserve 6 oz (175 g) of the icing for the decoration, then take four or five very small pieces of the icing, dip them in the reserved egg white and use them to fix the cake to the cake board. Now brush the almond icing all over with egg white and roll the fondant out to a square measuring 13½ × 13½ inches (34 × 34 cm). Lift it carefully with the aid of a rolling pin and transfer it to the cake, placing it centrally over it. Use a palette knife to smooth it over the top and down the sides and to round the corners. Don't worry about any gaps or holes because the fondant can be eased back together gently and smoothed over.

Decorated holly leaf cake (see above) and Ribboned parcel cake (see page 28).

Trim the base neatly all round then, if you need to, smooth the top and sides of the cake by sliding a palette knife all over each surface. Now dust the work surface again with icing sugar and roll out the remaining fondant (including the trimmings). Using the holly leaf cutter, stamp out the holly leaves – you will need 84 altogether so keep re-rolling the trimmings until you have enough.

Brush each one with egg white and arrange on the top and sides of the cake (see the photograph on page 26). To fix the silver balls, make up a 'cement' by mixing a heaped dessertspoon of icing sugar with a little cold water, put the merest trace in the centre of each arrangement of holly leaves, and fix three silver balls in place (the best way to to this is to use scrubbed eyebrow tweezers!). Now the cake is complete and can be stored in a container until needed.

If you are decorating an 8 inch (20 cm) round cake, you'll need 58 holly leaves and 116 silver balls. Make a circle of holly leaves, end to end, around the top edge of the cake and around the base, with another circle in the centre as well. Use 2 silver balls between each holly leaf.

NOTE: If you're using ready-made icing you'll need 1½ lb (700 g).

For a Ribboned Parcel Cake

Make up the icing as above, and roll it all out to cover the cake completely (without leaving any aside for trimmings). Then take 2 yards (2 metres) of any ribbon of your choice; red, green, silver or gold. In the photograph (see page 26) we used some silver metallic strips that have had sequins stamped out of them. These are available from dressmakers who specialise in weddings, and sometimes from florists.

First measure the lengths needed to make the parcel effect and fix these firmly, using large dressmaking pins with little bobbles on the ends. Then make the rest of the ribbon into a large bow and affix this in the same way. Store the cake in a large container till needed. Before serving be careful to remove the pins securing the ribbon.

GLACÉ FRUIT TOPPING

·

FOR AN 8 INCH (20 CM) ROUND OR A 7 INCH (18 CM) SQUARE CAKE

A t Christmas there are so many unusual glacé fruits available in the shops that seem to disappear at other times of the year. These can make very attractive alternative toppings for Christmas cakes. There are cherries (in all colours), glacé pineapples, peaches and I've even seen strawberries. You can, of course, use any combination you like. As you can see in the photograph on page 30, I've chosen dark glossy prunes to go with the russet colours of figs and apricots – there really couldn't be an easier or quicker way to top a cake. Just finish it off by tying it with a pretty Christmas ribbon. One point to note: the amounts of the fruits are approximate, since this will ultimately depend on how artistic you may or may not be.

8 no-soak prunes	1 heaped tablespoon apricot jam
6 no-soak apricot halves	2 tablespoons brandy
2 no-soak figs, halved	
5 glacé cherries (or any other combination of glacé fruits)	

First of all, heat the jam and the brandy together in a pan, whisking well until they are thoroughly blended. Then, using a brush, coat the surface of the cake quite generously with the mixture.

Next arrange the fruits in rows or circles on top of the cake, making as pretty a pattern as you can. Brush the fruits, again quite generously, with a coating of the glaze. Then cool the cake and store in a sealed container till needed. The brandy acts as a preservative and the topping will keep well (stored in a cool place) for several weeks. Don't worry about the keeping-quality of this glaze – we have stored glazed cakes for three months and they were still in beautiful condition.

GLAZED NUT TOPPING

·

This is suitable for all cakes but is specially good on the Creole Christmas cake (see page 18), which is too rich to cope with marzipan or even sweet icing.

45 pecan nut halves	1 heaped tablespoon apricot jam
15 whole Brazil nuts	2 tablespoons brandy
16 walnut halves	

First of all pre-heat the grill and lightly toast the pecans and Brazils, which not only gives them a better colour but a nicer flavour too. Be very careful though to watch them like a hawk: they really only need a couple of minutes if the grill is very hot and they should be pale gold rather than deep brown!

Whilst they're cooling, place the apricot jam and brandy in a small saucepan and heat them gently together, whisking until they're thoroughly blended. Now, using a brush, paint some of the mixture all over the surface of the cake. Then arrange the nuts in whatever pattern you like (see opposite). There's room for real artistic licence here, so if you're not that way inclined you could rope in someone else – this bit after all does not involve cooking, just purely artistic talent. Finally, brush all the beautifully arranged nuts with lots more glaze, then store the cake in a tin or polythene box until it's needed.

NOTE: For keeping-qualities see Glacé fruit topping (page 29).

Glazed nut topping (see above) and Glacé fruit topping (see page 29).

Talking Turkey . . . and Geese and Hams

It is advisable – essential, if you are going to get what you want – to order your Christmas meat or poultry in advance. Bargaining for a turkey on Christmas Eve may be a challenge, but does nothing for your peace of mind (and there will only be scraggy birds left, anyway). So once you have made your decision on your meat or poultry, put your order in as early as you can. But read these notes first to help you make a decision: many people are unaware of the choices that are available – or could be available if we, as consumers, made demands which would filter down through the retailer to the producer.

Turkey

There was a time when all the turkeys reared in this country were black-feathered. But, in the same way that white bread became a fashionable refinement, so did the white turkey. The so-called problem with black feathers is that after plucking they leave what we might nowadays call designer stubble on the flesh, and this apparently offended earlier sensibilities.

So turkey breeders set out to evolve a breed of white turkey, more aesthetic and plumper of breast, and the cycle started. Demand prompted mass-production and intensive rearing, which in turn meant that the turkeys were fattened too fast on unsuitable food, and were not hung properly. The result was a 'sliced-white' turkey with about as much character and flavour as a factory-baked loaf. When turkeys were water-cooled and went into the deep freezer having absorbed some of the water, it was not entirely surprising that some people gave up on turkeys altogether.

The good news is that of late we have seen a revival of interest in *flavour* and – more important – breeders who are prepared to return to the traditional methods of rearing. In my own area in East Anglia I have located a farm which still produces the Norfolk Black turkey:

it does not have the enlarged breast we have become used to but it does have a more pronounced and infinitely better flavour. In fact, although the breast meat doesn't look as plentiful on a Norfolk Black, the shape of the breastbone makes this deceptive: there is never any shortage of meat in our house at Christmas time. It is the connoisseur's choice and not what everyone might want, but my earnest hope is that more farmers will be encouraged to rear this breed.

Other turkey farms in my area have pioneered another breed of turkey in quite substantial quantities. It is called the Bronze, and is a cross between the Norfolk Black and the White, going a long way to bridge the gulf between good flavour and high meat yield (for the addresses of suppliers see page 218). These breeders, and others like them, are also rearing Whites in a less intensive way, giving the birds more time to mature and hanging them in the traditional manner.

So there's hope. And in the end perhaps the answer lies with us, the shoppers, who should insist on flavoursome turkey. We are always at the mercy of our suppliers, and if what you have is an intensively reared, unmatured bird there is not a lot you can add in the cooking.

Goose

Largely, I think, because of the production problems outlined above, more and more people are turning to goose – not just for Christmas but for entertaining from Michaelmas (the traditional time to eat goose) right up till Christmas. Geese do not take kindly to intensive rearing, so more and more farmers are producing large flocks of free-range birds fed naturally on grass and post-harvest stubble. Judy Goodman on her farm in Worcestershire, for instance, raises 1300 free-range birds each season and dispatches them all over the country (as do other farmers listed on page 218).

If you are ordering one from a local butcher or supplier, look out for that golden-yellow skin which is the sign that it has been grass-fed: pale whitish skin indicates some other type of feeding and rearing. An 11–12 lb (5–5.5 kg) bird is the ideal weight, and will serve eight people quite generously. Although (like ducks) geese have a substantial layer of fat under the skin, this melts during the cooking and acts as an excellent internal basting process. It helps to keep the meat moist and succulent, but if it is poured off as it escapes during the cooking, the meat will not become fatty.

Smoked and Cured Ham

Why is it, I wonder, that this nation which has such a proud tradition of smoking, curing and pickling hams is content to buy the square, water-pumped, bland variety? Even in the famous food halls of Harrods, I was told, this is the number one choice. Thankfully they also have enough discerning customers to stock a large range of traditional cures sold as half or whole hams on the bone. To get the very best flavour from your ham it is important to cook it on the bone – and of all the seasons of the year Christmas is the one that can justify the indulgence. The main cures to look out for are:

Marsh York cure: If you prefer an unsmoked ham, this is the finest. Mild cured and slowly matured, it has a sharp salty flavour. It happens to be the favourite of the ham buyer at Harrods (who comes from Yorkshire!), who recommends it be eaten with a good sharp English mustard that makes your nose wrinkle!

Bradenham cure: For those who enjoy a smoked ham. This has a very dark, almost black skin and a sweet subtle flavour which comes from being steeped in a mixture of spices, juniper berries and molasses before being smoked and matured.

Suffolk cure: Nigel Jerry (who helped us explore the salting and curing of hams in the TV series), together with his father, has a Royal Warrant for his superb hams. His Suffolk hams are first brined, then pickled in a mixture of stout, spices and molasses. They are then smoked over oak chippings and hung up to mature for several weeks. The skins are a rich mahogany colour and the care with which they are produced is certainly evident in their depth of flavour.

It is possible to order ready-cooked hams from many outlets all over the country (see page 218), but for myself there is nothing to touch the wonderful aroma of a ham baking in the oven at Christmas – all part of the ritual and anticipation of the festive season.

CHAPTER 2

Christmas Puddings

AND

Mincemeat

Stir up, we beseech thee, O Lord,
the wills of thy faithful people,
that they plenteously bringing forth
the fruit of good works, may
be of thee plenteously rewarded.

The prayer on the previous page, the Collect for the 25th Sunday after Trinity, has become synonymous with Christmas puddings and this particular day has long been known as Stir-up Sunday. The great cry 'stir up' was an apt reminder to all congregations to indulge in a bit of human stirring up and get the Christmas pudding made in plenty of time to mature before Christmas. The fruits of this particular good work, the currants, raisins and sultanas, not to mention the nuts, spices and alcohol, will indeed bring their reward – not in this case God's blessing, but instead (once they have all combined and matured) the greatest steamed pudding in the world.

There are those who profess to loathe Christmas pudding. In some cases I suspect they have never tasted the real thing. The average commercial version and, I have to say, many recipes in cookery books bear little resemblance: properly made Christmas pudding is *not* heavy or cloying, but a sumptuous combination of textures and flavours that have blended together. It is rich, yes, but a small quantity served with a smooth pouring sauce and some chilled dessert wine makes the perfect ending to a perfect meal.

Maturing: I think it is something of a myth that the longer you keep a pudding, the better it will taste. There is a definite limit and, in all honesty, I much prefer this year's Christmas pudding to last year's. The optimum maturing period is 6–8 weeks, so if you do find you have a pudding left over then I would advise you to *freeze* it for next year.

Heating and re-heating: I accept that the microwave is useful for many things, but *not* for re-heating steamed puddings. It may be more of a chore but conventional steaming is really very much better. If you have part of a pudding left after Christmas lunch (we usually have a 2 lb (1 kg) one left over) the best way to warm it up for Boxing Day is to wrap it in foil and re-heat in a medium oven for about 30 minutes.

Mincemeat: My views on mincemeat are similar to my reservations about Christmas puddings. Manufacturers offer us a vast range of mincemeats at different prices and in many quality ranges, but homemade mincemeat is so superior it ought to carry a consumer's warning: once you've made it at home, you'll never be able to buy it again!

TRADITIONAL CHRISTMAS PUDDING

·

SERVES 8 TO 10 PEOPLE

This recipe makes one large pudding in a 2 pint (1.2 litre) basin (see page 43). If you have any left over it will re-heat beautifully, wrapped in foil, in the oven next day. If you want two smaller puddings, use two 1 pint (570 ml) basins, but give them the same steaming time. I think it is best served with Rum sauce (see page 199).

4 oz (110 g) shredded suet	1 oz (25 g) almonds, skinned and chopped
2 oz (50 g) self-raising flour, sifted	1 small cooking apple, peeled, cored and finely chopped
4 oz (110 g) white breadcrumbs	
1 level teaspoon ground mixed spice	The grated zest of ½ large orange
¼ teaspoon freshly grated nutmeg	The grated zest of ½ large lemon
A good pinch ground cinnamon	2 eggs, size 1
8 oz (225 g) soft dark brown sugar	2½ fl oz (75 ml) barley wine
4 oz (110 g) sultanas	2½ fl oz (75 ml) stout
4 oz (110 g) raisins	2 tablespoons rum
10 oz (275 g) currants	
1 oz (25 g) mixed candied peel, finely chopped (buy whole peel if possible, then chop it yourself)	You will need a 2 pint (1.2 litre) pudding basin, lightly greased.

Begin the day before you want to steam the pudding. Take your largest, roomiest mixing bowl and start by putting in the suet, sifted flour and breadcrumbs, spices and sugar. Mix these ingredients very thoroughly together, then gradually mix in all the dried fruit, mixed peel and nuts followed by the apple and the grated orange and lemon zests. Don't forget to tick everything off so as not to leave anything out. Now in a smaller basin measure out the rum, barley wine and stout, then add the eggs and beat these thoroughly together. Next pour this over all the other ingredients, and begin to mix very thoroughly. It's now traditional to gather all the family round, especially the children, and invite everyone to have a really good stir and make a wish! The mixture should have a fairly sloppy consistency – that is, it should fall instantly from the spoon when this is tapped on the side of the bowl. If you think it needs a bit more liquid add a spot more stout. Cover the bowl and leave overnight.

Next day pack the mixture into the lightly greased basin, cover it with a double sheet of greaseproof paper and a sheet of foil and tie it securely with string (you really need to borrow someone's finger for this!) It's also a good idea to tie a piece of string across the top to make a handle. Place the pudding in a steamer set over a saucepan of simmering water and steam the pudding for 8 hours. Do make sure you keep a regular eye on the water underneath and top it up with boiling water from the kettle from time to time. When the pudding is steamed let it get quite cold, then remove the steam papers and foil and replace them with some fresh ones, again making a string handle for easier manoeuvring. Now your Christmas pudding is all ready for Christmas Day. Keep it in a cool place away from the light. Under the bed in an unheated bedroom is an ideal place. You'll find Christmas Day steaming instructions on page 199.

If you want to make individual Christmas puddings for gifts, this quantity makes eight 6 oz (175 g) small metal pudding basins (see page 219). Steam them for 3 hours, then re-steam for 1 hour. They look pretty wrapped in greaseproof paper and muslin and tied with attractive bows and tags.

NOTE: If you can't get barley wine (pubs usually have it), use extra stout instead. The best way to use what's left over, if you don't want to drink it, is to add it to a slowly cooked beef casserole to give it a beautiful rich sauce.

❖ ❖ ❖

CUMBERLAND RUM BUTTER

·

SERVES 8 PEOPLE

Cumberland rum butter is excellent not only with mince pies (see page 48) but also with the Light or Traditional Christmas puddings (see pages 37 and 39) or the Apple, mincemeat and nut strudel (see page 52).

6 oz (175 g) unsalted butter, at room temperature	6 oz (175 g) soft dark brown sugar
	6 tablespoons rum

You can either blend the butter and sugar together till pale, soft and creamy in a food processor or else use an electric hand whisk. When you have a pale smooth mixture you can gradually add the rum, a little at a time, beating well after each addition. Taste and add more rum if you think it needs it! Then place the butter in a container and chill thoroughly before serving. It is important, I think, to serve this very cold so that it can provide a wonderful contrast to the hot mince pies or pudding. It will keep for 2–3 weeks in the refrigerator so it's not really worth freezing.

Brandy Butter

Brandy butter is made in the same way, substituting brandy for the rum.

LIGHT CHRISTMAS PUDDING

·

SERVES 8 PEOPLE

If there are still people who claim not to like even our splendid Traditional Christmas pudding (see page 37), then this could be for them. It's a light sponge pudding containing mincemeat, chopped apple and mace so that the Christmassy flavour is there, and a very attractive arrangement of whole candied peel will look very pretty when it's turned out. The rather large quantity of booze, instead of going into the pudding, is used in what can only be described as a superlative Hot punch sauce (see page 40).

6 oz (175 g) self-raising flour, sifted	1 teaspoon lemon juice
A pinch salt	The grated zest of 1 small orange
4 oz (110 g) butter, softened	The grated zest of 1 small lemon
4 oz (110 g) soft light brown sugar	2 pieces whole candied orange peel
1 medium cooking apple, peeled, cored and chopped small	2 pieces whole candied lemon peel
	1 piece candied citron peel
2 eggs, size 1	
3 rounded tablespoons mincemeat	You will need a 2 pint (1.2 litre) pudding
⅛ teaspoon ground mace	basin – the rounded-based sort is best.

Prepare the basin by buttering it lightly and arranging the candied peel in the base. First snip the citron peel into ½ inch (1 cm) strips and arrange these in an overlapping circle in the centre of the base of the basin; you need something that resembles a flower. Then, using a sharp pair of scissors, snip the whole candied peels lengthways into strips, but leaving the end intact. Imagine five fingers attached to a hand and you've got it. Now arrange these around the 'flower', spreading out the strips as much as possible.

Now, for the pudding, simply beat the sugar and butter with an electric hand whisk until the mixture is pale and creamy and drops off a spoon easily with a sharp tap. Then beat the eggs in a jug and add these a minute amount at a time, whisking well after each addition. When all the liquid egg is incorporated carefully fold in the sifted flour, mace and salt, followed by the lemon juice, grated lemon and orange zest, chopped apple and finally the mincemeat.

Now spoon the mixture into the basin, being careful to leave your artistic arrangement intact. Tie a double piece of pleated foil on to the basin, place it in a steamer over boiling water and steam for 2½ hours.

When the pudding is completely cold you can turn it out, wrap it well and freeze it till needed.

Take it out of the freezer late on Christmas Eve and re-steam on Christmas Day for 1½ hours. Serve cut in slices with Hot punch sauce (see page 40).

HOT PUNCH SAUCE

SERVES 8 PEOPLE

This is a wonderful, very boozy sauce which, once tasted, makes you wonder why we ever bother to put alcohol in puddings. The sauce can be made well in advance, as long as you re-heat it gently and don't let it boil.

10 fl oz (275 ml) water	6 fl oz (175 ml) dry sherry
2 oz (50 g) caster sugar	(or medium will do)
The thinly pared outer rind of ½ medium orange	2 tablespoons rum
	2 tablespoons brandy
The thinly pared outer rind of ½ large lemon	1 rounded dessertspoon plain flour and 3 oz (75 g) unsalted butter worked together into a paste
The juice of 1 medium orange	
The juice of 1 large lemon	

Measure the water into a small saucepan, then cut the thinly pared orange and lemon rind into tiny shreds. Add them to the water along with the sugar, then gently bring the mixture up to simmering point and simmer gently for 20 minutes. Meanwhile, squeeze the orange and lemon juice into a bowl, and measure out the sherry, rum and brandy to join it. As soon as the 20 minutes are up, whisk the butter and flour paste into the contents of the saucepan. Bring back to simmering point, still whisking until the sauce has thickened. Now, keeping the heat very low, add the alcohol and fruit juices and, stirring gently, allow everything to become very hot without coming to the boil.

Serve some sauce spooned over each portion of pudding and hand the rest around separately.

HOMEMADE CHRISTMAS MINCEMEAT

·

MAKES 6 LB (2.75 KG)

*H*omemade mincemeat is dead simple to make. But in the past people used to have trouble storing it. This was because the high percentage of apples oozed too much juice and the juice started to ferment. In the following recipe the mincemeat is placed in a barely warm oven and so the suet gradually melts and as this happens it coats all the fruits, including the apples, sealing in the juices.

1 lb (450 g) Bramley apples, cored and chopped small (no need to peel them)	12 oz (350 g) soft dark brown sugar
	The grated zest and juice of 2 oranges
8 oz (225 g) shredded suet	The grated zest and juice of 2 lemons
12 oz (350 g) raisins	2 oz (50 g) whole almonds, cut into slivers
8 oz (225 g) sultanas	4 teaspoons mixed ground spice
8 oz (225 g) currants	½ teaspoon ground cinnamon
8 oz (225 g) whole mixed candied peel, finely chopped	Nutmeg, grated
	6 tablespoons brandy

All you do is combine the above ingredients, except for the brandy, in a large mixing bowl, stirring them and mixing them together very thoroughly indeed. Then cover the bowl with a clean cloth and leave the mixture in a cool place overnight or for 12 hours, so the flavours have a chance to mingle and develop. After that pre-heat the oven to gas mark ¼, 225°F (120°C), cover the bowl loosely with foil and place it in the oven for 3 hours.

Then remove the bowl from the oven and don't worry about the appearance of the mincemeat, which will look positively swimming in fat. This is how it should look. As it cools stir it from time to time; the fat will coagulate and instead of it being in tiny shreds it will encase all the other ingredients. When the mincemeat is quite cold stir in the brandy. Pack in clean dry jars, cover with wax discs and seal. It will keep in a cool, dark cupboard indefinitely, but I think it is best eaten within a year of making. For a classic traditional mince pie recipe see page 48.

NOTE: Vegetarians can make this mincemeat happily, using vegetarian suet.

◆-●-◆

LITTLE MINCEMEAT SOUFFLÉ PUDDINGS

·

SERVES 8 PEOPLE

*T*hese little soufflé-like puddings are what I would call very well-behaved! You can cook them in advance and re-heat them, and they will rise up again. You can even freeze them – and they will still be light and puffy. Serve them with Chilled rum sabayon (see page 44).

4 oz (110 g) butter	The grated zest of ½ lemon
4 oz (110 g) caster sugar	Extra butter and caster sugar for coating the moulds
6 eggs, size 1, separated	
6 oz (175 g) light gingercake, reduced to fine crumbs in a food processor	A little icing sugar for serving
A generous pinch ground cloves	You will need eight 3½ inch (9 cm) ramekin dishes.
¼ teaspoon ground cinnamon	
4 oz (110 g) mincemeat	

PRE-HEAT THE OVEN TO GAS MARK 4, 350°F (180°C)

First of all brush the ramekins with softly melted butter, then tip caster sugar around the inside of each mould to give an overall dusting. Tap out any excess sugar and arrange the ramekins in a shallow roasting tin.

Next, in a mixing bowl, cream the butter and 2 oz (50 g) of the sugar together until the mixture is pale and fluffy. Then beat in the egg yolks, a little at a time. Fold in the cake crumbs, followed by the spices, mincemeat and lemon zest.

Now, in a separate bowl, whisk the egg whites until they stand in soft peaks, and gradually whisk in the remaining 2 oz (50 g) sugar. What you will now have is a meringue mixture and this should be carefully folded into the rest. Spoon an equal quantity of the mixture into each ramekin, pour approximately ½ inch (1 cm) of boiling water into the roasting tin, then transfer it to the centre of the oven to bake for 25 minutes.

Turn the puddings out on to warm serving plates by sliding a palette knife round the edges, then tipping each one out upside down. Dust with a little sifted icing sugar and serve the Chilled rum sabayon separately.

NOTE: If you want to make these puddings ahead, they will re-heat at the same temperature in 15 minutes.

Traditional Christmas pudding (see page 37).

CHILLED RUM SABAYON

·

SERVES 8 PEOPLE

This whipped sauce made with egg yolks, sugar and alcohol is traditionally called sabayon by the French and zabaglione by the Italians. Either way it's light and fluffy and, served chilled, helps to avoid last-minute preparations.

4 egg yolks, size 1	2–3 tablespoon rum
2 oz (50 g) caster sugar	
4 tablespoons freshly squeezed orange juice	

Begin by placing a heat-proof bowl over a saucepan of barely simmering water (but don't let the bowl actually sit in the water). Then add the egg yolks and the sugar, and whisk together until frothy. Next add the orange juice and rum, and continue to whisk vigorously with a wire (or electric) whisk for about 8 minutes until the sauce is thick and foamy. Do not let the water under the bowl rise above a bare simmer during this time.

Remove the bowl from the heat. Cool, cover and chill thoroughly in the refrigerator. Taste before serving and, if you like, add some extra rum!

NOTE: This sauce is best made the day you actually need it – if kept overnight it does tend to separate.

ICED CHRISTMAS PUDDING *with* GLACÉ FRUITS

·

SERVES 8 PEOPLE

If you would like to offer your guests a frozen alternative to Christmas pudding, then this is unbeatable. It consists of creamy textured ice cream made with dark rum and creamed coconut, interspersed with chunks of glacé fruits that have been soaked in dark rum. What's more – and only because it's Christmas – there's an accompaniment of more glacé fruits soaked in Madeira (see page 46), which are spooned over the pudding just before serving!

FOR THE RUM-SOAKED FRUIT:
2½ oz (60 g) candied peel (orange, lemon and citron), cut into small chunks
1 oz (25 g) raisins)
3 glacé cherries, cut into quarters
6 tablespoons dark rum

FOR THE ICE CREAM:
4 egg yolks, size 1

4 oz (110 g) caster sugar
15 fl oz (425 ml) thick double cream
7 fl oz (200 ml) Greek yoghurt
1½ oz (40 g) creamed coconut, grated

You will need a 2½ pint (1.5 litre) pudding basin.

Marinate all the fruits in the rum overnight. Next day, in a bowl, whisk the egg yolks and sugar together. Then in a small saucepan bring the cream up to simmering point and add the grated coconut to it, stirring until the coconut has dissolved completely. Now pour the cream and coconut mixture on to the egg mixture, whisking all the time – it should thicken like light egg custard. Allow it to cool slightly before adding the yoghurt. Stir everything well and leave to get cold before adding the marinated fruits together with the rum.

Stir well again, then pour the whole mixture into the pudding basin, cover with cling film and place in the freezer until almost set – this is when the ice cream has the consistency of 'soft scoop', and it can take up to 7 hours to set to this stage. At this point stir it very thoroughly to distribute any ice crystals and make sure the fruits are evenly distributed. Return to the freezer overnight.

The ice cream will freeze, but still remain soft in texture. To turn it out, dip the bowl briefly in hot water, then slide a palette knife around the edge. Serve at once, cut into slices, with the Glacé fruits in Madeira (see page 46).

NOTE: Because this ice cream is soft in texture there is no need to remove it from the freezer in advance of serving. Any ice cream pudding left over after serving must be returned immediately to the freezer and taken out again for second helpings.

GLACÉ FRUITS *in* MADEIRA

·

This is a wonderfully alcoholic mixture of fruits steeped in Madeira (see opposite). The dry Sercial Madeira seems to give the best results. It's extremely handy to have a jar of this in the cupboard as an instant addition to spoon over any kind of ice cream, as well as the Iced Christmas pudding (see page 45).

4 oz (110 g) glacé cherries (red, green and yellow)	1½ oz (40 g) muscatel raisins
2 oz (50 g) glacé pineapple	Approximately 10 fl oz (275 ml) Sercial Madeira
4 oz (110 g) whole mixed candied peel	
1½ oz (40 g) crystallised ginger, finely chopped	You'll need a sterilised glass jar of 18 fl oz (500 ml) capacity.

Begin by chopping the candied peel and pineapple into approximate ½ inch (1 cm) squares – I think the fruit mixture should be quite chunky. Leave the cherries whole, but the ginger does need to be smaller than the rest as its flavour can be quite powerful. Now mix all the fruit together in a bowl.

Wash the jar in warm soapy water, rinse well and dry thoroughly with a clean cloth so that it's sparkling clean. Pack all the fruits into the jar (and try to give a good distribution of colour), then pour in the Madeira. Seal and leave, if possible, for 1 month before using. There's no need to refrigerate: the fruits will keep indefinitely as long as they're covered with the Madeira. One warning though: you'd better not eat these if you're driving!

◆━●━◆

Iced Christmas pudding with glacé fruits (see page 45) topped with Glacé fruits in Madeira (see above).

TRADITIONAL MINCE PIES

·

MAKES 24

I will always cherish fond memories of my mother's and my grandmother's cooling trays piled high with freshly baked mince pies on Christmas Eve, ready to be packed into tins and brought out whenever friends popped in for Christmas drinks. The following is the traditional family recipe.

12 oz (350 g) plain flour	FOR THE TOP:
3 oz (75 g) lard	A little milk
3 oz (75 g) margarine or butter	Icing sugar
A pinch salt	
Cold water to mix	You'll need one (or two) trays of 2½ inch
1¼ lb (560 g) mincemeat (see page 41)	(6 cm) patty tins, one fluted 3 inch (7.5 cm) pastry cutter and one 2½ inch (6 cm) cutter.

PRE-HEAT THE OVEN TO GAS MARK 6, 400°F (200°C)

Make up the pastry by sifting the flour and salt into a mixing bowl and rubbing the fats into it until the mixture resembles fine crumbs. Then add just enough cold water to mix to a dough that leaves the bowl clean. Leave the pastry to rest in a polythene bag in the refrigerator for 20–30 minutes, then roll half of it out as thinly as possible and cut it into two dozen 3 inch (7.5 cm) rounds, gathering up the scraps and re-rolling. Then do the same with the other half of the pastry, this time using the 2½ inch (6 cm) cutter.

Now grease the patty tins lightly and line them with the larger rounds. Fill these with mincemeat to the level of the edges of the pastry. Dampen the edges of the smaller rounds of pastry with water and press them lightly into position to form lids, sealing the edges. Brush each one with milk and make three snips in the tops with a pair of scissors. Bake near the top of the oven for 25–30 minutes until light golden-brown. Cool on a wire tray and sprinkle with icing sugar. When cool, store in an airtight tin.

◆–◆–◆

LATTICE MINCE PIES

Up in the English Lakes they serve a variation on the mince pie called a Cumberland Rum Nicky. These small pies are served hot with their tops lifted slightly away from the filling and some spiced Cumberland rum butter inserted to melt into the mincemeat. Now that I've discovered a useful little instrument called a lattice pastry-cutter (see page 219), I like to make my variation on the Rum Nicky, which is a mince pie with a lattice top that allows the rum butter to melt through the pastry when it is spooned over. The ingredients and baking times for this are the same as for Traditional mince pies. Follow the instructions for making the pastry, then make the lattice tops as follows.

Roll half the pastry out to approximately ⅛ inch (3 mm) thick and cut out two dozen 3 inch (7.5 cm) rounds to form the bases of the mince pies. Fill these with mincemeat and dampen the pastry edges with water. Now roll out the rest of the pastry into an oblong shape and cut the oblong into long strips 2½ inches (6 cm) wide, then use the lattice-cutter (A) to cut firmly along the length of each strip. Ease out the lattice (B), then stamp out the tops of the mince pies using the 2½ inch (6 cm) cutter (C). Any untidy edges will not show once the tops are in position and the edges sealed. Brush with milk and bake.

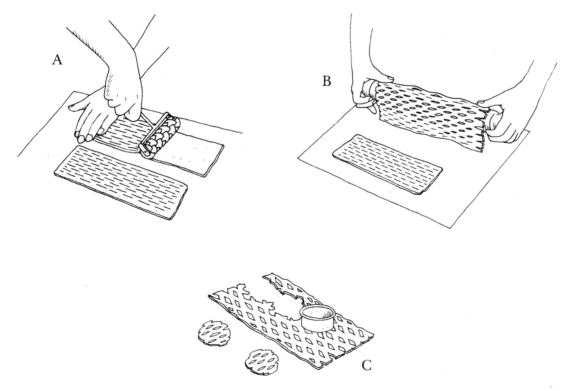

WHOLEFOOD MINCEMEAT SLICES

·

MAKES 12

These are a good alternative to mince pies made with pastry for those who (a) don't want to make pastry or (b) are wholefood-minded. They are very speedy to make and taste wonderful.

5 oz (150 g) vegetable margarine	8 oz (225 g) mincemeat
3 oz (75 g) soft brown sugar	
8 oz (225 g) wholewheat flour	You'll need a shallow baking tin 11 × 7
4 oz (110 g) porridge oats	inches (28 × 18 cm), well buttered.

PRE-HEAT THE OVEN TO GAS MARK 6, 400°F (200°C)

Start off by melting the margarine gently in a large saucepan, together with the brown sugar. While that's happening, mix the flour and porridge oats together in a mixing bowl.

When the margarine and sugar mixture has turned liquid and there are no lumps of fat or sugar lurking (give it a stir with a wooden spoon to get rid of them), remove the pan from the heat and begin adding the flour and oats to the pan, stirring well with each addition.

When it's all thoroughly blended, spoon half the mixture into the prepared tin. Now, using the flat of your hand, press the mixture down firmly all over, making sure it gets into all the corners. The firmer you press, the less crumbly the slices will be when they're cooked.

Next, using a tablespoon, spread the mincemeat evenly all over, pressing it out with the back of the spoon. Then spread the remaining oat mixture over the top, again pressing it down firmly and evenly all over.

Now bake the mixture in the centre of the oven for about 20 minutes or until the top is tinged brown. Then remove it from the oven and use a sharp knife to cut it into 12 squares, but leave them in the tin until they are quite cold. Then you can remove them more easily.

When they've cooled, lift them out with a palette knife and store in an air-tight tin – that's if they're not all eaten straight away.

◆ ◆ ◆

Apple, mincemeat and nut strudel (see page 52).

APPLE, MINCEMEAT *and* NUT STRUDEL

·

SERVES 8 PEOPLE

This is a Christmas party pud which will serve 8 people very generously; perfect for a buffet lunch (see page 50). Filo or strudel pastry is wonderful for storing in the freezer as you can just take out a few sheets as and when you need them (remember they take about 3 hours to thaw), and because there's no fat in it you can happily re-freeze what you don't use. If you hate making pastry and want something very simple to make – this is it!

4 Bramley apples, weighing about 1¼ lb (560 g) in total	2 oz (50 g) flaked almonds, lightly toasted under the grill
8 oz (225 g) mincemeat (see page 41)	1 oz (25 g) white breadcrumbs
The grated zest of 1 orange	4 sheets filo or strudel pastry (from a defrosted 1 lb (450 g) pack)
The grated zest of 1 lemon	
1 heaped tablespoon soft brown sugar	2 oz (50 g) unsalted butter
½ teaspoon ground mixed spice	Icing sugar
½ teaspoon ground cinnamon	
2 oz (50 g) pecan nuts, chopped and lightly toasted under the grill, or 2 oz (50 g) walnuts (but do not toast them)	You'll need a large heavy baking sheet 15 × 11 inches (37.5 × 28 cm), well greased.

PRE-HEAT THE OVEN TO GAS MARK 5, 375°F (190°C)

Begin by peeling and coring the apples and slicing them very thinly into a large bowl, sprinkling in the sugar as you slice. Then add the mincemeat, orange and lemon zest, spices and toasted pecan nuts and mix thoroughly.

In a small bowl combine the toasted almonds and breadcrumbs together. Then melt the butter. Now you are ready for the pastry, so remove your first sheet from the pack and arrange it over the baking sheet; it will overlap it but that doesn't matter. Brush the entire sheet with melted butter, then sprinkle one-third of the almond and breadcrumb mixture all over. Put the second sheet directly over the first and repeat exactly. Then the third sheet followed by the butter and the last of the almonds and breadcrumbs. Now put the last sheet of pastry on top of the rest, brush with the last of the butter, and place the apple and mincemeat filling all along the pastry lengthways in a band about 3½ inches (9 cm) wide, 3 inches (7.5 cm) from the edge of the baking sheet.

Now imagine you're making a giant sausage roll and begin by bringing one edge of the pastry leaves lengthways over the filling and the other edge up and over that. Turn the whole thing over so that the pastry join is underneath and place the strudel fairly centrally on the baking sheet. Now pinch the ends together and tuck them under, making a sausage about 14 inches (35 cm) long. Brush the whole surface with the remaining butter and bake in the centre of the oven for 40–45 minutes or until it turns a golden-brown. Cool the strudel for 15 minutes, then dust it thickly with icing sugar and serve cut in slices with, best of all, Cinnamon ice cream (see page 170) or chilled whipped cream.

◆━●━◆

LATTICE MINCEMEAT DESSERT TART

·

SERVES 8 PEOPLE

*H*ere is another festive dessert that makes good use of homemade mincemeat. Serve it fairly warm, with Cumberland rum butter (see page 38) to melt through the lattice.

10 oz (275 g) plain flour	FOR THE TOP:
2½ oz (60 g) butter or margarine	A little milk
2½ oz (60 g) lard	Icing sugar
Cold water to mix	
1¼ lb (560 g) homemade mincemeat (see page 41)	You'll need a 9 inch (23 cm) quiche tin, lightly greased.

PRE-HEAT THE OVEN TO GAS MARK 6, 400°F (200°C)

After making up the pastry (see Traditional mince pies, page 48), place it in a polythene bag and leave it to rest in the refrigerator for 20 minutes or so before rolling out. Then cut off one-third of the pastry and reserve it (for the top), roll out the remaining two-thirds and use it to line the prepared tin. Spoon the mincemeat over the pastry, spreading it out evenly with a palette knife. Using a pastry brush, dampen the edge of the pastry all round.

To make the lattice top, roll out the remaining pastry to an oblong strip measuring approximately 10 × 7 inches (25 × 18 cm), then run a lattice-cutter along the length of the pastry, pressing *firmly* as you go, and continue in parallel over all the oblong. Now gently ease out the lattice, using both hands to pull it open. When it is fully opened you will have a 10 inch (25 cm) square which needs to be lifted gently on to the pie. Press the lattice edges gently against the pastry lining, then trim off the excess all round. Brush the lattice with milk and bake the tart on a baking sheet on the highest shelf of the oven for about 20–30 minutes. Dust the tart with icing sugar before serving, and hand round the chilled Cumberland rum butter (see page 38) separately.

CHAPTER 3

Preserves, Pickles AND Chutneys

*H*ere's a good example of nature organising matters very conveniently for Christmas. In this country we have a long tradition of pickling and preserving the fruits of late summer and autumn – which then mature beautifully in time to accompany the array of cold cuts, the ham, pork, tongue and so on, without which no Christmas eating programme would be complete. But it does seem to be a peculiarly British tradition – I once gave a jar of homemade chutney to a French family I was visiting, and they were totally bewildered by it!

The recipes in this section should cover most eventualities and are pretty versatile: there are things to accompany good old bread and cheese or sausage rolls, to give a touch of class to left-overs, to complement hot dishes, even to use as ingredients in sauces. I have provided quantities for just one jar of each variety because I think it's nicer to have a selection over Christmas. On the other hand, preserves make marvellous Christmas presents (especially if you can shop around for attractively-shaped jars and make little Christmas 'hats' for them with ribbons and labels – see the photograph on page 59 – in which case the ingredients in all recipes can be doubled or trebled as required.

Jars: Always put pickles and preserves in spanking-clean jars that have been washed in warm soapy water, then rinsed and dried with a clean cloth and sterilised in a medium oven for 5 minutes. Pour in the contents while they are still hot.

Sealing: It's a good idea to cover chutney with a waxed paper disc and, if you are not using proper preserving jars, with a rubber seal. Be careful of metal lids as the vinegar can make them corrode very quickly (plastic lids like those on top of instant coffee jars are the best of all). Cellophane or paper coverings are not to be recommended, as they can cause the vinegar to evaporate and the chutney to sink.

Spices: Several recipes in this book call for 'mixed pepper berries'. These are a mixture of black, white, pink and green peppercorns with allspice berries (pimento) included as well. They are available at most supermarkets, but are sometimes called different names.

SPICED PICKLED PEARS

·

MAKES A 1¾ PINT (1 LITRE) JAR

Pears in a mild spicy pickle make a wonderfully new and different accompaniment to Christmas cold cuts or, if you warm them through slightly, they are magic with either a roast duck or a goose. They look very pretty and appealing too, as they turn a lovely amber colour and make an excellent homemade Christmas gift (see page 59). If you want to make more simply double or treble the recipe and so on, remembering that 2 lb (1 kg) pears fills a 1¾ pint (1 litre) jar.

2 lb (1 kg) Conference pears (pick out the hardest, smallest ones you can find)	½ teaspoon whole cloves
12 oz (350 g) soft light brown sugar	1 level teaspoon juniper berries
10 fl oz (275 ml) white wine vinegar	1 level dessertspoon mixed pepper berries (see opposite)
10 fl oz (275 ml) cider vinegar	
A 3 inch (7.5 cm) cinnamon stick, broken into 3 pieces	You will need a 1¾ pint (1 litre) preserving jar.
½ lemon, cut into thin slices	

Start off by putting all the ingredients except the pears in a large saucepan and place it on a low heat, allowing it to come slowly to the boil. Give everything a whisk round from time to time to dissolve the sugar crystals. While that's happening peel the pears. They need to be pared very thinly (forgive the pun). This means using either a very sharp knife or, best of all, a really good potato parer. Take off all the peel but leave the stalks and the base florets intact. As you peel each pear plunge it into a bowl of cold water. Then, after peeling them, check that the sugar has completely dissolved into the vinegar, drain the pears and add them to the saucepan. Bring everything up to a gentle simmer and let the pears cook for about 20 minutes or until they look slightly transparent and feel tender when tested with a small skewer.

Using a draining spoon, transfer the pears and slices of lemon to the clean sterilised preserving jar (see page opposite). Now boil the syrup furiously for about 5 minutes until it's reduced to approximately 15 fl oz (425 ml) and pour in enough to fill the jar right up to its neck and completely cover the pears. Then scoop out the spices and add them to the jar as well. Any left-over syrup can be discarded. Cover and seal the jar and, when the contents are completely cold, wipe and label it and store it in a cool dark place for about 1 month before using. The pears will keep well for 6 months.

◆◆

PICKLED SHALLOTS *in* SHERRY VINEGAR

·

MAKES A 1¾ PINT (1 LITRE) JAR

*O*ne Christmas tradition in our family is returning from Midnight Mass to freshly baked crisp sausage rolls and equally crisp pickled onions. I have now discovered that pink shallots with a little sherry vinegar make a different, rather special version. They do tend to disappear rather quickly, I find, so if you can bear to peel them why not make double the quantity below?

1 lb (450 g) pink shallots, peeled	¾ teaspoon whole mixed pepper berries
1 pint (570 ml) water	(see page 56)
2 oz (50 g) salt	
4 fl oz (110 ml) sherry vinegar	You will need a 1¾ pint (1 litre)
10 fl oz (275 ml) white wine vinegar	preserving jar.

You need to begin 2 days ahead by placing the shallots in a 2 pint (1.2 litre) bowl. Then mix the water and salt together, pour this over the shallots and leave them covered with a cloth for 2 days.

When you're ready to start pickling, bring the vinegars and mixed berries up to simmering point in a saucepan, then leave them to get quite cold. Meanwhile drain the shallots in a colander, pat them dry with kitchen paper, then pile them into a 1¾ pint (1 litre) sterilised preserving jar (see page 56). Pour the cold vinegar (plus the spices) into the jar, seal it tightly and leave in a cool place for 1 month before eating.

◆━●━◆

Spiced pickled pears (see page 57), Spiced preserved tangerines (see page 62) and Pickled shallots in sherry vinegar (see above).

SPICED APRICOT *and* ORANGE CHUTNEY

·

MAKES A 1¾ PINT (1 LITRE) JAR

This is a superlative chutney: it makes an elegant accompaniment to the Terrine with four cheeses (see page 94), is excellent with Pheasant terrine (see page 120), and is the main ingredient for a wonderful sauce for Roast loin of pork (see page 128).

14 oz (400 g) no-soak apricots	2 cloves garlic, finely chopped
1 teaspoon whole coriander seeds	1 level tablespoon salt
8 oz (225 g) soft light brown sugar	½ teaspoon cayenne pepper
15 fl oz (425 ml) cider vinegar	The grated zest and juice of 1 small orange
1 medium onion, chopped	
2 oz (50 g) sultanas	
2 tablespoons finely grated fresh root ginger	You will need a 1¾ pint (1 litre) preserving jar.

Begin by chopping the apricots into smallish chunks, then place them in a sieve and rinse them under cold water. Shake off the excess water and put them in a large saucepan.

Now place the coriander seeds in your smallest saucepan and heat the pan whilst tossing the seeds around it – as soon as they begin to splutter transfer them to a pestle and mortar and crush them lightly before sprinkling them over the apricots. Add all the remaining ingredients to the apricots, then heat gently, stirring all the time until the sugar crystals have dissolved. Next bring everything up to simmering point and simmer the chutney (covered) for 45 minutes–1 hour. The apricots and onion need to be quite tender, but it's important not to overcook the chutney or it will be too thick – the right consistency is like chunky rather than liquid jam. Remember, too, that it does thicken as it cools down.

When it's ready, spoon into the warmed, sterilised jar (see page 56) and seal straightaway, and label when cold. This is best kept for 1 month before eating.

◆ ◆ ◆

CHRISTMAS CHUTNEY

·

MAKES A 1¾ PINT (1 LITRE) JAR

This is so-named because it is made with dried fruits, which I always associate with Christmas: prunes, dates and apricots. It's dark, spicy and delicious with cold cuts, pork pies or hot sausages – and it goes splendidly with matured Cheddar or the Terrine with four cheeses (see page 94).

12 oz (350 g) pitted no-soak prunes	2 oz (50 g) sea salt
10 oz (275 g) pitted dates	3 oz (75 g) allspice berries
10 oz (275 g) dried apricots	1 lb (450 g) demerara sugar
1 lb (450 g) onions, peeled	
1 pint (570 ml) cider vinegar	You will need a 1¾ pint (1 litre)
1 dessertspoon grated fresh root ginger	preserving jar and a small piece of muslin
or 1 heaped teaspoon ground ginger	or gauze.

The dried fruits and the onions need to be chopped very small, and this can be done in a food processor or with an old-fashioned mincer, or else with a sharp knife and lots of patience!

When they're all dealt with, put the vinegar in a large saucepan with the salt and the ginger, then tie the allspice berries up in a small piece of muslin or gauze very securely so they can't escape and add these to the pan. Bring everything up to the boil, then stir in the chopped dried fruits and onions together with the sugar. Leave it all to simmer very gently without a lid for about 1½ hours, or until the chutney has thickened. Stir it from time to time during the cooking period. When it's ready you will be able to draw a spoon across the surface of the chutney and make a trail that doesn't immediately fill up with surplus vinegar.

Spoon the cooked chutney into warmed sterilised jars (see page 56), seal well with waxed discs and tight lids, and label as soon as it's cold. Keep this chutney for 1 month to mature before eating.

◆ ● ◆

SPICED PRESERVED TANGERINES

·

MAKES AN 18 FL OZ (500 ML) JAR

What is a tangerine?, we have to ask ourselves nowadays: the word seems to apply to a whole variety of species. I have made this particular preserve with one called Suntina (from Israel), and with another variety called Mineola (see page 59). Both of them make a remarkably good preserve for serving with cold ham, tongue, goose and game. Gently heated, this also makes a splendid accompaniment to roast duck or venison.

Approximately 1½ lb (700 g) small tangerine-type oranges	1 level teaspoon whole cloves
1 pint (570 ml) water	2 blades mace
8 fl oz (225 ml) white wine vinegar	¾ teaspoon mixed pepper berries (see page 56)
8 oz (225 g) soft light brown sugar	
A 2 inch (5 cm) cinnamon stick, broken into pieces	You will need an 18 fl oz (500 ml) preserving jar.

First of all wash the oranges and wipe them dry, then slice them thinly into ¼ inch (5 mm) thick round slices (you'll have to discard the end pieces, which are just peel). Place them in a saucepan with the water, bring them up to simmering point and simmer very gently for about 45 minutes or until the oranges are quite tender.

Now drain them in a large sieve fitted over a bowl (so you can reserve all the cooking liquid). Next return the cooking liquid to the saucepan along with the wine vinegar, sugar and spices. Boil the mixture rapidly for about 10 minutes and, after that, return the orange slices to the pan and this time simmer gently for a further 20 minutes or until the slices look translucent.

Transfer the orange slices to a warmed, sterilised jar (see page 56), then once again boil the syrup until it has reduced to about 10 fl oz (275 ml). Now pour the warm syrup, including the spices, on to the oranges, but don't seal the jar because any leftover syrup can be added after 24 hours, by which time the oranges will have absorbed some of the syrup. Seal and label, and store for at least a month before eating (but not more than 3 months).

◆—◆—◆

PICKLED BEETROOT *with* SHALLOTS

·

MAKES AN 18 FL OZ (500 ML) JAR

Beetroot is vastly underestimated, in my opinion. Perhaps that's because the strong malt vinegar of the commercial pickling masks the true flavour of the beetroot, or maybe it's because of overboiling. But when prepared in the following way it provides a wonderfully flavoured and textured accompaniment to cold cuts at Christmas time.

1 lb (450 g) raw beetroot	½ teaspoon crushed rock salt
2 shallots	
½ teaspoon mixed pepper berries (see page 56)	You will need an 18 fl oz (500 ml) preserving jar.
6 fl oz (175 ml) red wine vinegar	

PRE-HEAT THE OVEN TO GAS MARK 5, 375°F (190°C)

Trim the beetroot and wipe them, but leave the skins on. Then wrap them all up together in a parcel of foil. Place the parcel on a baking sheet and bake them for about 3 hours or until they feel tender when pierced with a skewer. Now remove them from the oven and, as soon as they are cool enough to handle, peel off the skins and slice them thinly.

Peel and slice the shallots thinly too, then layer the beetroot and shallots in the sterilised jar (see page 56). Next place the vinegar, berries and salt in a small saucepan, bring up to simmering point, and pour the whole lot straight over the beetroot and shallots to cover them completely. Seal the jar immediately, label it when cold, then store. The beetroot doesn't need to mature – it can be eaten within a day or two and will keep well, provided it is always totally immersed in the vinegar (so you may need to top it up after you use some).

—◆—◆—

Christmas on Ice?

I have to admit there was a time when the idea of freezing ahead for Christmas offended my idealistic views: not only was it a cop-out, but the flavour of the food was bound to be affected. Time, and the experience of cooking for the family, have modified these ideals somewhat. Far better to acknowledge that the freezer does have its place in Christmas preparations, and can help to ease the pressure on the cook, than finish up a nervous wreck on Christmas Eve!

What I have set out below is a guide to what can usefully be frozen in advance. But first let me enter two words of caution. Not everything fares well in the freezer – it has to be used selectively (and anyway it doesn't have a bottomless capacity). Also, I still feel that the secret of successful freezing lies in not freezing anything too long. Therefore most of the experiments done for this book involved no more than 4–6 weeks' freezing.

Brandy or rum butter: Although these keep perfectly well in the fridge for up to 2 weeks, any further ahead than that they should be frozen in rigid containers.

Bread: All kinds of bread will freeze well – rolls, freshly baked French sticks (cut these in half for easier packing and pack in sealed polythene bags), family loaves, Walnut and raisin bread (see page 92) or Quick cheese, sage and onion bread (see page 100).

Breadcrumbs: These will be needed for Traditional bread sauce (see page 197) and stuffings, or for coating Ham hash cakes (see page 211). A good supply laid in early will save you hunting around for a 2-day-old loaf at the last minute.

Butter: Very often an imponderable. If you're not sure how much you will need, store a few extra packs, including Normandy or unsalted for serving with cheese.

Canapé bases: Cheese pastry, croustades and baked croûtons all freeze extremely well packed in sealed containers.

Casserole: Do you need to plan a casserole for supper on Christmas Eve when there will be precious little time for extra cooking? Decide now and put it in the freezer in a foil container with a cardboard lid.

Cheese: One thing I have discovered after years of trying to serve soft cheeses, such as Camembert, Brie or Reblochon, at the ripe, creamy stage without them going over the top is that if you buy them at the critical moment, wrap them in foil and freeze (for up to 1 month), when defrosted they will return to their perfect degree of readiness quite unimpaired.

Chestnuts (fresh): Because these are so tedious to peel, you would do well to save your temper by not attempting the job when the Christmas pressure is on. Peel them (see page 213) and either freeze them raw in a sealed bag, or else cook them, then mash and freeze ready for the stuffing.

Cranberries: You can shop early for your cranberries as they do freeze well. Spread them on a tray and seal in a polythene bag.

Croûtons: Made just a couple of weeks in advance, these can be stored without freezing in sealed jars or tins. Otherwise freeze them in sealed polythene bags, and thaw by spreading them out on a baking sheet in a hot oven for about 10 minutes (for recipes see pages 86, 209 and 212).

Dates (fresh): Dried dates are a must at Christmas, but the fresh ones also taste wonderful with cheese and nuts. Freeze them in sealed polythene bags.

Fish: Sometimes, after the excesses of Christmas, it's nice to end the holiday with some fish – my own preference is for smoked haddock (ready for an Omelette Arnold Bennett, see page 216). Pack in sealed polythene bags, but first check with your fishmonger that it hasn't already been frozen.

Ice creams: What could be nicer than a supply of ice creams (see pages 170–3), made well ahead and ready to serve? Make sure you remove the one you want to the main body of the fridge 30–40 minutes before serving (20–30 minutes for a sorbet).

Ice cubes: The party season will call for lots of ice cubes for drinks. You can either fill polythene ice bags with still mineral water (tap water may cloud the cubes), or else buy a big bagful from your local off-licence.

Lemon, lime or orange slices (for drinks): Extremely handy to have ready prepared for drinks like gin and tonic, Campari or vermouth. Scrub the fruit well, slice into rounds and then into halves, spread them out on trays to open-freeze, then place these in sealed polythene bags.

Mince pies: These can be frozen (uncooked) in well-greased patty tins, then removed with a palette knife and stored in sealed foil containers or polythene bags. Return them to the patty tins for baking from frozen at gas mark 7, 425°F (220°C), for about 30 minutes. You can also freeze cooked mince pies and refresh them in a warm oven when defrosted.

Pastry: All pastry freezes well, so why not have portions of shortcrust or cheese pastry ready for tarts or quiches? I also like to have a quantity of Quick flaky pastry in the freezer for using with left-overs (see page 72).

Sausage rolls: These can be frozen (raw), packed between layers of greaseproof paper, then cooked from frozen. Brush with beaten egg and cook in a pre-heated oven at gas mark 7, 425°F (220°C), for about 30 minutes.

Stuffings and sauces: All sauces (with the exception of hollandaise) *can* be frozen, but the end-product is never quite as good as the original. I also feel that any stuffing should be put into the turkey at room temperature; if it is not very thoroughly defrosted it can cause problems (not least the worry of getting it defrosted in sufficient time), and I believe freezing is there to ease worry not add to it!

Recipes Suitable for Freezing (up to 4 weeks)

Apple, mincemeat and nut strudel
Braised pheasants in Madeira
Brandy butter
Bûche de Noël (before decorating)
Canapé bases
Cheese choux pastries filled with mushrooms in Madeira (freeze filling and pastry separately)
Cheese pastry
Cinnamon ice cream
Coffee and hazelnut macaroons
Cumberland rum butter
Fig ice cream
Homemade chocolate truffles
Iced chocolate chestnut creams
Iced Christmas pudding
Lattice mincemeat dessert tart
Light Christmas pudding

Little mincemeat soufflé puddings
Little sticky toffee puddings
Mulled wine sorbet
Parmesan-baked parsnips (coated but not cooked)
Quick cheese, sage and onion bread
Sausage rolls
Savoury cheese palmiers with ham and anchovies
Stollen
Tiny cheese, onion and olive scones
Traditional braised red cabbage with apples
Traditional mince pies
Truffle torte
Vegetarian 'sausage rolls'
Walnut and raisin bread
Walnut shortbreads

CHAPTER 4

Canapés
AND
Nibbles

When it comes to parties the cook at Christmas is faced with a paradox; because it's Christmas you have to serve something rather special, but because it is Christmas the time in which to be creative and special is severely limited. Over the years, I have tried to find that happy balance between sweat and tears, and creativity. You cannot avoid spending time on preparing food for larger numbers of people – the secret is not to be doing it when they are ringing the doorbell.

This is the reason why I often opt for the least complicated form of party, a drinks party, and why the recipes in this section are designed to need the minimum of last-minute attention and special equipment. Canapés have come on a long way in recent times; the old limp asparagus in aspic has given way to some very imaginative little bites (being offered by top chefs and party caterers at upwards of £3.50 a mouthful!).

The recipes below are based approximately on multiples of one dozen. How many canapés you want to serve to guests is up to you – with the proviso that the more you make, the more will disappear! My own rule of thumb is to offer six to eight different 'nibbles', which can, if necessary, be supplemented by crisps, nuts, olives, etc. If, when you have multiplied this by the number of guests, it sounds like a daunting number, remember that the bases and pastry cases can be made well in advance and frozen, and fillings can be added nearer the time. And one more consolation: there won't be mounds of greasy washing-up to do in the small hours. You might even get an early night!

◆–●–◆

PITTA BREAD CANAPÉS *with* PÂTÉ *and* PICKLED CUCUMBER

·

MAKES 12

These little canapé bases are extremely crisp and thin. They really couldn't be easier or quicker, and topped with the pâté and pickled cucumbers (or gherkins) they provide crispness, gutsy flavour and crunch all in one lovely mouthful!

FOR THE BASES:
1 white or wholemeal pitta bread

1 generous teaspoon olive oil

1 clove garlic, crushed

FOR THE TOPPING:
12 slices pickled cucumber

2 oz (50 g) chicken liver pâté mixed with a few drops brandy

You will need a solid baking sheet, spread with the olive oil and garlic, and a 1¼ inch (3 cm) pastry cutter.

PRE-HEAT THE OVEN TO GAS MARK 4, 350°F (180°C)

All you do is split open the pocket of the pitta bread lengthways with a sharp knife so that you have two separate halves. Now put the bread halves (baked sides uppermost) on a board or work surface and stamp out little rounds using a 1¼ inch (3 cm) pastry cutter, giving each one a sharp tap as you cut – don't twist the cutter or you won't get perfect rounds.

As you cut them out, place them on the baking sheet touching but not overlapping; you should get at least 12 rounds in all and the birds will love the crumbs from the trimmings. Now bake the rounds for about 15 minutes on a high shelf in the oven till they are crisp and golden. Cool them on a wire rack and store them in a screw-top jar or airtight tin until you're ready for them. They can be made several days in advance.

When you need to serve them, spread each one with pâté and top with pickled cucumber.

Alternative toppings from the supermarket are:
hummus with black olives
taramasalata with green olives and cayenne
smoked mackerel pâté with capers

◆ ◆ ◆

MUSHROOM *and* QUAIL EGG TARTLETS *with* HOLLANDAISE

·

MAKES 12

These are the most delicious little bites imaginable. Quail eggs are the perfect size for canapés: if you can't get hold of them, though, you could use some finely chopped hen's eggs piled on top of the mushroom filling and finished off with hollandaise. Because you only need a small amount of cheese pastry, I suggest you make up the Cheese pastry on page 89, use a quarter of it for these canapés and freeze the rest for some other time. Alternatively you can make 48 canapé cases and freeze some for another occasion.

¼ quantity Cheese pastry (see page 89)	1 small clove garlic, crushed
	1 teaspoon lemon juice
FOR THE MUSHROOM FILLING:	Salt and freshly milled black pepper
¼ oz (or half a 15 g packet) dried porcini mushrooms (available from delicatessens or Italian shops)	TO FINISH:
	6 quail eggs
4 oz (110 g) fresh mushrooms, finely chopped	½ quantity Quick blender hollandaise (see page 207)
1 shallot, finely chopped	
1 oz (25 g) butter	You'll also need a tray of tiny tartlet tins,
1 tablespoon fresh chopped parsley	brushed with melted butter, and a 2¼ inch (5.5 cm) fluted pastry cutter.

PRE-HEAT THE OVEN TO GAS MARK 5, 375°F (190°C)

Make up the pastry cases by rolling out the pastry on a lightly floured working surface to a thickness of no more than ⅛ inch (3 mm). Using a 2¼ inch (5.5 cm) fluted cutter, cut out pastry rounds and push these gently into the small tartlet tins. Prick the bases with a fork, then bake on a high shelf for 10–15 minutes until golden and crisp. Cool on a wire rack and store in an airtight container.

To make the mushroom filling, first put the porcini mushrooms in a small bowl and pour in sufficient boiling water to cover them generously. Then leave on one side to soak for 30 minutes. Towards the end of this time, heat the butter in a frying-pan and when it's foaming add the shallot and garlic, and cook over a low heat for 8–10 minutes or until softened. Now drain the water from the dried mushrooms and use your hands to squeeze all the excess moisture out of them. Chop these finely, then stir them into the frying-pan along with the fresh mushrooms and turn up the heat. Cook gently until the moisture has evaporated, leaving a thick spreadable mixture – this will take 20–25 minutes. Then add the parsley, cook for 1 minute more and remove the pan from the heat. Flavour with lemon juice, salt and freshly milled pepper.

While that's happening you can be dealing with the quail eggs. It is best to have them at room temperature before boiling them gently for 5 minutes. Pour off the hot water and cool the eggs under a cold running tap. Gently crack the shells, then peel carefully: this is a slow job so put some nice music on.

When it is time to assemble the canapés, warm the tartlet shells briefly in a moderate oven for about 5 minutes – and warm the mushroom mixture as well (if it is not already warm). Spoon the mushroom mixture into the tartlet shells, top with half a quail egg, and finish off with just enough hollandaise spooned over to cover the top of each tartlet.

◆◆◆

MOZZARELLA *and* TOMATO APPETISERS

·

MAKES 12

These are simple but very effective. Try to get a good quality Italian Mozzarella, though, and remember the amount of cheese will vary according to the size of the tomatoes.

12 cherry tomatoes	Approximately 3 oz (75 g) fresh
Approximately 1 tablespoon Italian pesto sauce (a pinenut and basil sauce sold in jars)	Mozzarella cheese, cut into 12 cubes
	Salt and freshly milled black pepper

You will need 12 cocktail sticks.

First cut the tomatoes in half and scoop out and discard all the seeds. Then spread out a sheet of kitchen paper and leave them turned upside down on it for about 15 minutes so that they can drain a little. Finally, to assemble them, turn them right way up, spoon a little pesto sauce into each half and impale it through its base on a cocktail stick, push a piece of Mozzarella along to join the cut side and then follow it with another half of tomato, its cut side joining the Mozzarella. Lay them all on a serving plate and sprinkle with a little salt and freshly milled black pepper before serving.

NOTE: If you make these in advance, don't put them in the refrigerator as this tends to spoil the flavour.

SAUSAGE ROLLS

·

MAKES ABOUT 24

M ade with a melting quick flaky pastry, these are one of our major treats at Christmas. They can be prepared well in advance, frozen uncooked and then defrosted and baked from the freezer on Christmas Eve or whenever you need them.

FOR THE QUICK FLAKY PASTRY:	1 lb (450 g) good quality pork
8 oz (225 g) plain flour	sausagemeat
6 oz (175 g) butter or block margarine	1 teaspoon dried sage
A pinch salt	1 egg, beaten, to glaze
Cold water to mix	

You will need 2 baking sheets, lightly greased.

FOR THE FILLING:
1 medium onion, grated

PRE-HEAT THE OVEN TO GAS MARK 7, 425°F (220°C)

The fat needs to be rock-hard from the refrigerator, so weigh out the required amount, wrap it in a piece of foil, then return it to the freezing compartment for 30–45 minutes. Meanwhile sift the flour and salt into a mixing bowl. When you take the fat out of the freezer, open it up and use some of the foil to hold the end with. Then dip the fat in the flour and grate it on a coarse grater placed in the bowl over the flour. Keep dipping the fat down into the flour to make it easier to grate.

At the end you will be left with a pile of grated fat in the middle of the flour, so take a palette knife and start to distribute it into the flour (don't use your hands), trying to coat all the pieces of fat with flour until the mixture is crumbly. Next add enough water to form a dough that leaves the bowl clean, using your hands to bring it all gently together. Put the dough into a polythene bag and chill it for 30 minutes in the refrigerator.

When you're ready to make the sausage rolls mix the sausagemeat, onion and sage together in a mixing bowl. Then roll out the pastry on a floured surface to form an oblong (as thin as you can). Cut this oblong into three strips and divide the sausagemeat also into three, making three long rolls the same length as the strips of pastry (if it's sticky sprinkle on some flour).

Place one roll of sausagemeat on to one strip of pastry. Brush the beaten egg along one edge, then fold the pastry over and seal it as carefully as possible. Lift the whole thing up and turn it so the sealed edge is underneath. Press lightly, and cut into individual rolls each about 2 inches (5 cm) long. Snip three Vshapes in the top of each roll with scissors and brush with beaten egg. Repeat all this with the other portions of meat and pastry.

If you are going to cook straightaway, place the rolls on baking sheets and bake high in the oven for 20–25 minutes. If you want to cook them later, store them uncooked in a freezer box and freeze until needed. Although you can store the cooked and cooled sausage rolls in an airtight tin, they do lose their crunchiness. For this reason I think it is preferable to remove a few at a time from the freezer and cook them as required.

MULLED WINE

·

SERVES 12 PEOPLE

The following recipe has been donated by Alice King, the Daily Mail's *wine correspondent and Drinks Editor of* Marie Claire *and* Best *magazines. Alice says that the great thing about mulled wine is that you can keep adding to it. If unexpected guests arrive and you've no wine left, simply add some more water and fruit. Use the recipe below as a basic guideline, adjusting the quantities of wine if you want it stronger and adding more sugar or honey if you like it sweeter.*

2 × 75 cl bottles medium to full-bodied red wine (Bulgarian Cabernet Sauvignon is ideal)	6 tablespoons granulated sugar or honey
2½ pints (1.5 litres) water	2 inch (5 cm) piece of cinnamon stick
1 orange stuck with cloves	2 teaspoons finely grated fresh root ginger or ground ginger
2 oranges, sliced	2 tablespoons fruit liqueur such as Cointreau, Grand Marnier or cherry
2 lemons, sliced	brandy (optional)

Put all the ingredients in a saucepan, then heat to simmering point, stirring until all the sugar has dissolved. Keep it barely at simmering point for at least 20 minutes – but do not boil or all the alcohol will evaporate. This can be made in advance, then re-heated just before the party. Serve it warm in ½-pint mugs (in which case there will be 12 servings) or else in 24 sturdy wine glasses.

BRUSCHETTAS *with* GOAT'S CHEESE, BASIL *and* TOMATO

·

MAKES 12

*T*his recipe is simplicity itself, but it has a wonderful combination of flavours and a very crunchy texture. If you're lucky enough to get hold of some fresh imported basil leaves to tear up and scatter on top, they'll be even better – these now come into the supermarkets, usually from Israel, in the winter months.

1 small slim French loaf – sometimes called baguettine	Approximately 2 oz (50 g) mild, creamy goat's cheese (the spreadable kind that comes in tubs is fine)
Good quality olive oil	
1 clove garlic, crushed	Rock salt and freshly milled black pepper
1 tablespoon Italian pesto sauce (a pinenut and basil sauce sold in jars)	Fresh basil leaves
2 firm medium-sized tomatoes	You will need a baking sheet, spread with about 1 tablespoon olive oil and the garlic

PRE-HEAT THE OVEN TO GAS MARK 4, 350°F (180°C)

First slice the bread into thinnish rounds; you won't need all the loaf. Now arrange the slices on the baking sheet, press them into the oil then turn them the other way up so that each surface has a slight coating of garlicky oil. Bake them in the centre of the oven for 20–25 minutes, or until they have turned a golden-brown and become very crisp. Do watch the timing on this – I have thrown away more burnt croûtons of bread than I care to remember! Cool them on a wire rack and store in an airtight tin until you need them (they will be OK for up to 2 weeks, which is very helpful).

When you're ready to serve, skin the tomatoes by pouring boiling water over them, soak for 5 minutes, then halve them, scoop out the pips, slip off the skins and chop the flesh into tiny dice. Now simply spread each crisp bread slice first with a thin layer of pesto, then with a generous layer of goat's cheese, and sprinkle on the diced tomato together with a little crushed rock salt and coarsely ground black pepper. Finally, using a small teaspoon, add a few droplets of olive oil – though be careful not to overdo this. If you do have a few fresh basil leaves to scatter over the bruschettas, so much the better, but if not they will still taste very good indeed.

◆—◆

TINY CHEESE, ONION *and* OLIVE SCONES

·

MAKES ABOUT 28

These are so moreish that I don't think your guests could possibly survive on just one. They are simple to make and freeze superbly once cooked, provided you defrost and re-heat them in a hot oven for about 4 minutes before serving. If you're making them on the day of serving, split them once they're cooled and spread with a little herb cheese or a creamy blue Italian cheese like Cambazola. Warm them in a hot oven just before serving.

6 oz (175 g) self-raising flour	1½ oz (40 g) strong Cheddar cheese, grated
1 medium onion, diced	
1 tablespoon olive oil	Approximately 2–3 tablespoons milk
½ teaspoon salt	1 egg, size 1
½ teaspoon mustard powder	6 black olives, stoned and chopped
½ teaspoon cayenne pepper	
Freshly milled black pepper	You will need a baking sheet, lightly greased, and a 1¼ inch (3 cm) plain pastry cutter.
1 oz (25 g) butter	
1½ oz (40 g) Parmesan cheese, grated	

PRE-HEAT THE OVEN TO GAS MARK 6, 400°F (200°C)

Fry the onion in the oil over a highish heat for about 5–6 minutes or until it's a nice brown caramel colour and darkened at the edges. Keep it moving about so that it doesn't burn. Now transfer it to a plate to cool.

While that's happening, take a large mixing bowl, sift in the flour, salt, mustard powder and cayenne and add a good grinding of black pepper (the scones need to have a piquant bite). Now rub in the butter, toss in the cooled onion, the olives and two-thirds of the grated cheeses, forking them in evenly. Beat the egg and pour this in, mixing first with a knife and finally with your hands, adding only enough milk to make a soft dough – it mustn't be too sticky. Turn the dough out on to a lightly floured surface, knead it gently till it's smooth, then roll it out to about ¾ inch (2 cm) thick, being careful not to roll it too thinly. Next, use a 1¼ inch (3 cm) plain cutter for cutting: place it lightly on the dough and give a sharp tap to stamp out the scones. Lightly knead together and re-roll any trimmings. Then, when all the scones are cut, brush them with milk, top them with the remaining grated cheese and bake them near the top of the oven for 10–12 minutes. Remove them to a wire rack to cool.

SAVOURY CHEESE PALMIERS *with* HAM *and* ANCHOVIES

·

MAKES 24 OF EACH

These little heart-shaped crisp savoury pastries are a delight to serve with drinks (see page 79). You can, if you like, make them 24 hours ahead, store in an airtight container and re-crisp them in a hot oven for a few minutes just before serving. If you want to freeze them uncooked and bake just before you need them then I suggest you use chopped black olives instead of anchovies which don't freeze satisfactorily.

6 oz (175 g) bought puff pastry	1 oz (25 g) tinned anchovies in oil, drained, or 12 stoned black olives, finely chopped
1 oz (25 g) strong Cheddar cheese, finely grated	1 oz (25 g) Parma ham or Pancetta is best, if you have an Italian shop in your area
1 oz (25 g) Parmesan cheese, freshly grated	
Freshly milled black pepper	You will need 2 large baking sheets, well buttered.

PRE-HEAT THE OVEN TO GAS MARK 7, 425°F (220°C)

This sounds a lot more complicated than it is: it's actually very simple (see below). Begin by assembling all the filling ingredients so that they're ready to use. Combine the cheeses together, then roll out the pastry to an oblong strip measuring 12 × 8 inches (30 × 20 cm). Now sprinkle the cheese on top of two-thirds of the pastry strip and add a good grind of black pepper. Next fold the

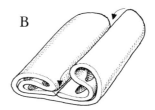

C

bottom third of the pastry, the bit without any cheese, over the centre third. Press the cheese very firmly into the remaining third and bring that up and over the other two-thirds. Then press the edges firmly with a rolling pin all round and roll the whole lot out to a square, this time measuring 8 × 8 inches (20 × 20 cm). Now cut the square in half so that you have two strips.

On one strip lay two-thirds of the Parma ham and on the other strip lay two-thirds of the anchovy fillets at intervals all along. Then fold each strip, bringing one end over to the centre and the other end to meet it (A). Arrange the rest of the ham and anchovies on the top of the folded-over sections. Then yet again bring the outside ends to the centre so that you are left with two rolls of four layers of pastry joined to each other in the centre (B). Gently pinch the pastry join together. Then take a sharp knife and cut the whole thing into ¼ inch (5 mm) strips (C). Lay these cut-side up on baking sheets, leaving a little gap all round so that they have room to expand. Now bake them for 10 minutes or until golden brown. Then cool on a wire rack.

◆ ● ◆

LITTLE CROUSTADES *filled with* GRAVADLAX *and* SOURED CREAM

·

MAKES 12

*A*gain these are simplicity itself and the filling comes from the supermarket. The croustades are made in mini tartlet tins which are available in trays of 12; what they are essentially are croûtons made into tartlet cases. There are a number of fillings that could go into them – the Guacamole and Anchoïade in my **Complete Illustrated Cookery Course** *(pages 340 and 406 respectively) are excellent.*

FOR THE CROUSTADES:	FOR THE FILLING:
3 slices medium cut bread (a light pale rye bread is excellent for this)	4 oz (110 g) gravadlax, finely chopped
2 oz (50 g) butter	3 tablespoons soured cream or Greek yoghurt
1 clove garlic, crushed	Cayenne pepper
Salt and freshly milled black pepper	

You will need a tray of tiny tartlet tins and a 2¼ inch (5.5 cm) plain pastry cutter

PRE-HEAT THE OVEN TO GAS MARK 4, 350°F (180°C)

Begin by placing the slices of bread on a flat surface and rolling them with a rolling pin to make them as thin as possible. Next stamp out rounds using a 2¼ inch (5.5 cm) plain cutter. Melt the butter in a small pan containing the garlic and a seasoning of salt and freshly milled black pepper.

Now brush the little bread rounds on both sides with melted butter and then press them into the tins firmly. Bake them for about 15–20 minutes or until crisp and brown. Cool them on a wire rack and store them in an airtight tin for up to 2 weeks.

To fill them for serving, simply pile the finely chopped gravadlax into each one and top with a little of the sauce that comes with it. Add a blob of soured cream and a dash of cayenne.

NOTE: Smoked salmon can be used just as effectively as gravadlax, in which case you add a little lemon juice before the soured cream.

We have found that, once assembled, these keep crisp for up to 3 hours.

◆—◆—◆

Savoury cheese palmiers with ham and anchovies (see page 76).

A Party Selection

Christmas entertaining can encompass a whole range of scenarios, from a few friends dropping in for drinks, to buffet lunches and fork suppers, and various kinds of dinner party. What I have set out here are a few ideas and guidelines for parties involving recipes from this book. Check the quantities in specific recipes: if the recipe serves 8, you will need one and a half times the quantity for 12 people. See the index to find the recipes below.

DRINKS PARTY
for 12 people

Choose any four of the canapé recipes and double the quantities, to provide eight canapés per person

VEGETARIAN BUFFET PARTY
for 12 people

Vegetarian 'sausage rolls'
Roasted red peppers stuffed with fennel

A terrine with four cheeses (double the recipe) with Spiced apricot and orange chutney
Broccoli salad with sesame dressing
Walnut and raisin bread (2 loaves)
Individual pecan pies with whipped cream
Compote of prunes in port with Fig ice cream
Cheese, fruit and nuts

CHRISTMAS DINNER PARTY
for 8 people

Roasted red peppers stuffed with fennel
Quick cheese, sage and onion bread
Roast stuffed goose with prunes in Armagnac (or with potato, sage and apple stuffing and Spiced pickled pears)
Traditional braised red cabbage with apples
Roast potatoes
A terrine with four cheeses with Christmas chutney
Mulled wine sorbet *or* Iced chocolate chestnut creams with white chocolate sauce

HOT FORK SUPPER
for 12 people

Caramelised cheese and onion tartlets (as a first course or in case one or two vegetarians are present)
Venison (or beef) with port, Guinness and pickled walnuts
Purée of potato and celeriac with garlic
Traditional braised red cabbage with apples
Champagne jellies with syllabub cream
Truffle torte
Walnut and raisin bread with a selection of cheeses
Fruit, nuts and crème de menthe jellies

BUFFET LUNCH PARTY
for 12 people

Bruschettas with goat's cheese, basil and tomato
·
Old-fashioned raised game pie
·
Cumberland sauce (or Cranberry and onion confit)
·
Salt-crusted mini baked potatoes with cold chive hollandaise
·
Four star slaw
·
Broccoli salad with sesame dressing
·
Christmas dried fruit compote
·
Apple, mincemeat and nut strudel
·
Quick cheese, sage and onion bread (2 loaves)
·
Cheese, fruit and nuts

NEW YEAR'S EVE CELEBRATION
for 8 people

Omelette Arnold Bennett, served in sections, with watercress
·
Traditional roast sirloin of beef with Yorkshire pudding
·
Roast potatoes
·
Parmesan-baked parsnips
·
Brussels sprouts
·
Cheese, nuts in the shell, muscatel raisins with port
·
Old English port wine jellies and/or Little sticky toffee puddings with pecan toffee sauce

HOT SPICED CIDER *with* ROASTED APPLES

·

MAKES 16 GLASSES

A glass of something warm and spicy goes very well with warmed mince pies during the party season (even though we no longer seem to greet guests rubbing frosty fingers and shaking snow off their boots)!

4 pints (2.25 litres) still dry cider
8 oz (225 g) soft brown sugar
24 whole cloves
8 whole cinnamon sticks
16 allspice berries
The juice of 2 oranges
½ whole nutmeg, grated
8 small Cox's apples
2 oz (50 g) butter

PRE-HEAT THE OVEN TO GAS MARK 5, 375°F (190°C)

First, using a small sharp knife, make a small slit around the 'waist' of each apple, then rub each one with butter. Place them on a baking sheet and bake in the oven for 20–25 minutes – they should be softened but not floppy, so test them with a skewer. Put all the other ingredients into a large saucepan and heat the mixture, stirring quite often and adding the apples halfway through. Don't let it come right up to the boil, but serve it very hot.

To keep it really hot without boiling it's probably best to use a simmering mat under the pan, then when you're ready to serve pour it into a large warmed bowl. Ladle into glass beer tankards with handles (spoons in the glass will prevent cracking).

CHAPTER 5

A Vegetarian Christmas

This chapter was inspired by a letter I received some time ago from a vegetarian who complained that he couldn't face yet another 'nut roast' Christmas, and please could I come up with some dishes that could accommodate all the Christmassy things like stuffings and sauces that add to the sense of occasion.

There was the challenge, and I have to say it hasn't been easy. But having had the support and critical approval of my various vegetarian friends (including Jackie who worked with us on the TV series), and after much tasting and enthusing, I feel sure all the recipes below more than hold their own for a Christmas feast.

My main consideration has been to assemble all the elements of a vegetarian Christmas lunch, and I have set out suggested menus below. However, I would add that if your family party contains only one or two vegetarians, there is advice on freezing on page 64 so that you can prepare the dishes ahead and be spared having to cook two different lunches at the same time.

—— MENU 1 ——
A Terrine with four cheeses, served with Spiced apricot and orange chutney and warm Walnut and raisin bread

•

Cheese choux pastries filled with mushrooms in Madeira, served with a mixed leaf salad

•

Compote of prunes in port, served with Fig ice cream

•

Fresh chilled dates, muscatel raisins and nuts in the shell, served with port

•

Coffee and Homemade chocolate truffles

—— MENU 2 ——

Roasted red peppers stuffed with fennel, served with Quick cheese, sage and onion bread

•

Cheese and parsnip roulade with sage and onion stuffing, served with Bread sauce or Cranberry and orange relish

•

Apple, mincemeat and nut strudel, served with Cinnamon ice cream

•

Potted cheese, served with nuts and muscatel raisins

•

Coffee and Homemade chocolate truffles

—— MENU 3 ——

Celery soup with blue cheese served with croûtons

•

Caramelised cheese and onion tartlets with Cranberry and orange relish, served with Broccoli salad with sesame dressing

•

Little sticky toffee puddings with pecan toffee sauce

•

Potted cheese with celery and oat cakes

•

Coffee and Homemade crème de menthe jellies

•

(See index for page numbers of these recipes)

◆━◆━◆

CELERY SOUP *with* BLUE CHEESE

·

SERVES 6 PEOPLE

This is really good made with a creamy blue cheese like the Irish Cashel Blue, but if you can't get hold of that a blue Wensleydale would also be good.

1 lb (450 g) celery (1 large head, trimmed weight)	5 oz (150 g) blue cheese (see above), rind removed and crumbled
2 oz (50 g) butter	Salt and freshly milled black pepper
1 potato (about 7 oz, 200 g), peeled and diced	FOR THE CROÛTONS:
1 pint (570 ml) vegetable stock (see page 207)	4 oz (110 g) thickly sliced white bread, crusts removed and cut into small cubes
1 small onion, finely chopped	4 tablespoons walnut oil
5 fl oz (150 ml) single cream	

First of all separate the stalks of celery from the base and trim, reserving the leaves for a garnish – the trimmed stalks should weigh 1 lb (450 g). Scrub them in cold water, drain them, then slice across into thinnish slices.

Now in a large saucepan melt the butter and stir in the celery, the chopped potato and the onion. Stir everything around to get a good coating of butter, then put a lid on the pan and, keeping the heat at minimum, allow the vegetables to sweat for ten minutes to release their buttery juices. Then uncover and pour in the stock and bring it up to simmering point. Cover again and cook gently for 30 minutes: after that test that the vegetables are tender and, if not, re-cover and continue to cook until they are.

Next remove the pan from the heat and stir in the cream, then liquidise the soup along with the crumbled cheese until it is quite smooth. Return the soup to the rinsed-out pan and re-heat very gently (because the soup, at this stage, should not be boiled). Taste and season with salt and pepper and serve the soup sprinkled with the chopped celery leaves and crisp croûtons (made by heating the walnut oil in a large frying-pan and frying the cubes of bread in it until golden-brown).

◆ ● ◆

WILD MUSHROOM *and* WALNUT SOUP

·

SERVES 8 PEOPLE AS A FIRST COURSE

Walnuts are at their best at Christmas time and, together with some dried wild mushrooms, can be used to make an unusual soup for a dinner party or a warming lunch or supper snack with some good cheese to follow.

1 oz (25 g) dried porcini mushrooms (available from delicatessens or Italian shops)	2 cloves garlic, crushed
	3½ pints (2 litres) hot water
	Salt
10 fl oz (275 ml) boiling water	
2 oz (50 g) butter	TO FINISH:
4 oz (110 g) open-cap mushrooms	8 oz (225 g) small open mushrooms – keep
2 medium carrots, chopped	4 whole and chop the rest finely
2 celery stalks, chopped	1 oz (25 g) butter
1 medium onion, chopped	4 oz (110 g) walnuts, ground in a nut mill
1 leek, washed and chopped	or food processor
2 bayleaves	3 fl oz (75 ml) single cream
1 teaspoon chopped fresh	3 fl oz (75 ml) dry sherry
or ¼ teaspoon dried thyme	1 dessertspoon lemon juice
¼ teaspoon dried sage	Salt and freshly milled black pepper

First place the dried mushrooms in a jug with 10 fl oz (275 ml) boiling water and leave them to soak for 30 minutes. Meanwhile in a very large saucepan melt the 2 oz (50 g) butter, then add all the prepared vegetables and herbs, stir well over a gentle heat until everything is glistening with a coating of butter, then pour in the dried mushrooms and their soaking water, followed by 3½ pints (2 litres) hot water. Add some salt, then bring up to a gentle simmer and, keeping the heat low, let the soup barely simmer for 1 hour.

After that, place a colander over a large bowl and strain the soup into it. Remove the bayleaves, and purée the vegetables with a little bit of the stock in a liquidiser or processor, then return this to the rest of the stock and whisk to a smooth consistency. Now wipe out the soup saucepan with some kitchen paper and return it to the heat with the 1 oz (25 g) butter. Lightly sauté the chopped mushrooms for about 5 minutes. After that, pour in the soup mixture, stir in the ground walnuts, season with salt and pepper, and let it continue cooking gently for 10 minutes. While that's happening use your sharpest knife to slice the 4 reserved whole mushrooms into wafer-thin slices for a garnish.

When you are ready to serve the soup, stir in the cream, sherry and lemon juice and serve piping hot with the slices of raw mushroom floating on top.

BROCCOLI CREAM CHEESE SOUP

·

SERVES 6 TO 8 PEOPLE

This is a pale, creamy soup with just a hint of cheese. Its light green colour makes it look most attractive when you serve it. I think it goes particularly well with buttered oatmeal biscuits or oat cakes.

1 × 8 oz (225 g) head broccoli	1 × 6 oz (150 g) packet low-fat (9%) soft cheese
1 medium onion, chopped	
2 whites of leek, rinsed and chopped	2 tablespoons fine oatmeal
1½ oz (40 g) butter	1 pint (570 ml) milk
1 pint (570 ml) vegetable stock (see page 207)	Salt and freshly milled black pepper

First trim the broccoli into tiny florets of approximately ¼ inch (5 mm), fanning them out to remove any dust and grit, then chop the stalky parts quite small as well. Now in a large saucepan melt the butter, add the chopped leeks, onion and broccoli stalks (leave aside the florets for later), stir well, then cover the pan and leave the vegetables to sweat for 10 minutes.

Next stir in the oatmeal, then add the milk, a little at a time, stirring well after each addition (as if you were making a sauce). When all the milk is in, add the stock and some seasoning, whisk well, then simmer gently for a further 10 minutes. After that, turn off the heat and allow the soup to cool a little. While that's happening steam the little florets over simmering water for exactly 4 minutes.

Now pour the soup and the soft cheese into a food processor or liquidiser to blend until smooth. Then return the soup to the rinsed-out pan, add the broccoli and re-heat gently. Taste to check the seasoning before serving.

◆–◆–◆

CARAMELISED CHEESE and ONION TARTLETS

·

MAKES ABOUT 8

These little tartlets are a splendid offering for vegetarian guests at any party. You can make the cases and the filling in advance, then just put them together and bake them on the day, and serve them warm from the oven.

FOR THE CHEESE PASTRY:	½ teaspoon mustard powder
6 oz (175 g) plain flour	3 oz (75 g) Gruyère cheese, grated
3 oz (75 g) butter, at room temperature	1 oz (25 g) butter
2 oz (50 g) strong Cheddar cheese, grated	2 large Spanish onions, finely chopped
½ teaspoon mustard powder	Cayenne pepper
A pinch cayenne pepper	Salt and freshly milled black pepper

FOR THE FILLING:	An eight 4 inch (10 cm) patty (or Yorkshire
2 eggs, size 1, beaten	pudding) tins ¾ inch (2 cm) deep, greased,
6 fl oz (175 ml) single cream	and a 5 inch (13 cm) pastry cutter.

PRE-HEAT THE OVEN TO GAS MARK 4, 350°F (180°C)

First make up the pastry by rubbing the butter lightly into the flour, then adding the cheese, mustard and cayenne plus just enough cold water to make a smooth dough. Then place the dough in a polythene bag to rest in the refrigerator for 20 minutes. After that roll it out as thinly as possible and use a 5 inch (13 cm) cutter or a saucer or similar item to stamp out eight rounds. Line the greased tins with them, then bake in the oven for 15–20 minutes or until the pastry is cooked through but not too coloured. Then cool them on a wire rack and store in an airtight tin until needed. Meanwhile, for the filling, melt the butter in a pan and cook the onions very gently, stirring often, for about 30 minutes or until they have turned a lovely golden-brown caramel colour. Cool and keep till needed.

To bake the tartlets: brush a little beaten egg on each pastry case and pre-bake them (same temperature as above) for 5 minutes – this helps to provide a seal for the pastry and stops it becoming soggy. Now mix the beaten eggs with the mustard and cream in a jug and season with salt and pepper. Next spoon the onion mixture into the cases and top that with grated cheese. Finally pour in the egg mixture and sprinkle with a little cayenne. Bake for 30 minutes or until puffy and golden. Stand in their tins for 10 minutes and serve warm.

CHEESE CHOUX PASTRIES FILLED *with* MUSHROOMS *in* MADEIRA

·

SERVES 2 PEOPLE

This is definitely a recipe that would serve two vegetarians handsomely at the Christmas lunch table. The three different kinds of mushroom are cooked very slowly in Madeira and then sandwiched between light cheese choux pastry. A good accompaniment would be a salad of mixed leaves, watercress and orange segments, dressed with a lemon vinaigrette.

FOR THE CHOUX PASTRY:	6 oz (175 g) open-cap mushrooms, roughly chopped
5 fl oz (150 ml) cold water	
2 oz (50 g) butter, cut into small pieces	6 oz (175 g) oyster mushrooms, roughly chopped
2½ oz (60 g) strong plain flour	
2 eggs, size 1, well beaten	6 oz (175 g) onions, finely chopped
2½ oz (60 g) Gruyère cheese, grated	1½ oz (40 g) butter
½ teaspoon mustard powder	2 cloves garlic, crushed
A pinch cayenne pepper	½ teaspoon chopped fresh thyme
Salt and freshly milled black pepper	3 fl oz (75 ml) double cream
Extra beaten egg to glaze	5 fl oz (150 ml) Sercial Madeira
	3 fl oz (75 ml) hot water
FOR THE FILLING:	Freshly grated nutmeg
1 × ½ oz (15 g) packet dried porcini mushrooms (available from delicatessens or Italian shops)	Salt and freshly milled black pepper
	A few sprigs watercress to garnish

You will need a solid baking sheet.

PRE-HEAT THE OVEN TO GAS MARK 6, 400°F (200°C)

You can make the filling for this and the raw choux pastry the day before, if you care to, as they can be assembled and cooked later without any ill-effects.

So for the filling: put the dried mushrooms in a jug and cover them with the hot water, then leave them to soak for 30 minutes. To make the sauce, melt the butter in a medium-sized saucepan and soften the chopped onions and garlic in it till pale gold (about 5 minutes). Then stir in all the fresh mushrooms, followed by the soaked mushrooms (snipped a bit with a pair of scissors if they're large) together with their soaking water. Season with salt and pepper and add the thyme and a few good gratings of nutmeg. Now pour in the Madeira, cover the pan with a tight-fitting lid and let the mushrooms cook as slowly as possible for 1½ hours: the liquid should barely simmer, and you should check it from time to time to make sure it hasn't evaporated.

When you are ready to make the choux pastries put the cold water in a medium-sized saucepan together with the pieces of butter, and leave it on one side while you weigh out the flour. Since you are going to need to 'shoot' the flour quickly into the water and melted butter, fold a sheet of greaseproof paper to make a crease, then open it up again. Sift the flour straight on to the square of greaseproof paper and season it with salt and pepper.

Now place the saucepan of water and butter over a moderate heat, and stir with a wooden spoon. As soon as the butter has melted and the mixture comes up to the boil, turn the heat off immediately, then tip the flour in (all in one go) with one hand while you beat the mixture vigorously with the other (you can do this with a wooden spoon, though an electric hand whisk would be much easier).

Beat until you have a smooth ball of paste that has left the sides of the pan clean (probably less than 1 minute), then beat the beaten eggs in, a little at a time, mixing each addition in thoroughly before adding the next, until you have a smooth glossy paste. Then add 2 oz (50 g) of the grated cheese, the mustard powder and a seasoning of salt and cayenne.

Next grease a good solid baking sheet and take heaped teaspoonfuls of the choux pastry and stack them closely together to form two circles roughly 5½ inches (14 cm) in diameter.

Brush each ring with beaten egg, then sprinkle them with the rest of the cheese. Place them on a high shelf of the oven and bake for 10 minutes. After that raise the temperature to gas mark 7, 425°F (220°C), and continue baking for 20 minutes. When the choux pastries are cooked, slit them in half horizontally. Stir the cream into the mushroom filling, then divide this between the two choux halves. Place the other two halves on top, put a few sprigs of watercress in the centre of each for colour, and serve as soon as possible.

◆•◆

WALNUT *and* RAISIN BREAD

·

MAKES A 1 LB (450 G) LOAF

I think one of God's greatest gifts to man is good cheese, and it deserves good bread to go with it. This chunky, slightly sweet bread goes extremely well with a sharp, vigorous Cheddar or fresh goat's cheese. It also freezes very well.

5 oz (150 g) strong wholewheat flour	7 fl oz (200 ml) hand-hot water
5 oz (150 g) plain flour	4 oz (110 g) walnut pieces
1 slightly rounded teaspoon salt	2 oz (50 g) muscatel raisins or lexia raisins
1 teaspoon walnut oil	2 oz (50 g) sultanas
1 slightly rounded teaspoon dried yeast	
1 teaspoon brown sugar	You will need a 1 lb (450 g) loaf tin, brushed with oil.

PRE-HEAT THE OVEN TO GAS MARK 6, 400°F (200°C)

Begin by combining the flours and salt together in a mixing bowl, and leave them to warm slightly in a low oven for 10 minutes. Meanwhile set the yeast to froth: start off by measuring 3 fl oz (75 ml) hand-hot water in a measuring jug, whisk in the sugar followed by the yeast, then leave on one side for 10–15 minutes until a good 1 inch (2.5 cm) head of froth has formed on the surface.

Next tip the yeast liquid into the warmed flour, followed by a further 4 fl oz (120 ml) of hand-hot water and 1 teaspoon of walnut oil. Mix to form a dough, adding a further tablespoon or two of water if it appears too dry: it should have the sort of consistency that leaves the side of the bowl clean and yet not be so soft that it clings to your hands and sticks to the work surface.

Now turn the dough out on to a lightly floured work surface and knead for 5 minutes – try to avoid using any additional flour because, as you knead, the dough will become less sticky and more bouncy. Press the dough out into a rough 12 inch (30 cm) square, and sprinkle the dried fruit and nuts over the surface. Roll up the dough, Swiss-roll style, then knead briefly again to distribute the fruit and nuts evenly. Now pat it out into an oblong, fold one edge into the centre and the other edge over that. Transfer the dough to the tin, and tap the tin on the work surface to settle the dough in but leave a nicely rounded top. Now put the tin inside an oiled plastic bag, trapping a little air inside to balloon the bag up out of contact with the surface of the dough. Then leave this in a warm place for about 1¼ hours or until the dough has risen to about 1½ inches (4 cm) above the edge of the tin.

Remove the risen loaf from the bag and transfer it to the centre of the oven to bake for 35 minutes. Slide a knife around the edge of the tin (as some of the dried fruit can stick to the tin), then turn the loaf out on to an oven-gloved hand and tap the base. The loaf should sound hollow – if it doesn't put it back in the oven for 5 more minutes, upside down without the tin. Cool on a wire rack.

◆-■-◆

VEGETARIAN 'SAUSAGE ROLLS'

•

MAKES 36

*T*he 'sausages' in these are in fact what the Welsh call Glamorgan sausages, which are a *mixture of cheese and herbs. These make delicious party snacks and go well with the chutney recipes (see pages 55–63). There is also a supermarket brand of chilli, garlic and ginger sauce which makes a lovely dipping sauce for these!*

1 quantity Quick flaky pastry, made with 8 oz (225 g) flour and 6 oz (175 g) butter (see page 72)	1 large onion, grated
	3 tablespoons thick double cream
Beaten egg to glaze	1 tablespoon fresh chopped herbs (chives, parsley, thyme, etc.)
	1½ teaspoons mustard powder
FOR THE FILLING:	A pinch cayenne pepper
10 oz (275 g) fresh breadcrumbs	Salt and freshly milled black pepper
8 oz (225 g) mature Cheddar cheese, grated	
	You will need 3 baking sheets, lightly greased.

PRE-HEAT THE OVEN TO GAS MARK 7, 425°F (220°C)

For the filling, simply place all the filling ingredients in a mixing bowl, season well and mix very thoroughly. Then turn to page 72 and follow the instructions for making conventional sausage rolls (except in this case it's nice to cut the rolls obliquely so that they form little diamond shapes). Snip each one on the top in three places with the end of some scissors, then brush with beaten egg. Bake, on greased baking sheets, on the top shelf of the oven for 20–25 minutes. Then leave them to cool on a wire rack before storing in an airtight tin (that is, if they're not all eaten before you get the chance)!

NOTE: These can be frozen before cooking. They can then be glazed and cooked from frozen for about 30–35 minutes.

93

A TERRINE *with* FOUR CHEESES

·

SERVES 8 PEOPLE AS A FIRST COURSE

This is a real winner: easy to make, it's superb to eat, and can be served as a starter, with a salad, or as a light snack. I love to serve it with Spiced apricot and orange or Christmas chutneys (see pages 60 and 61), and Walnut and raisin bread (see page 92). My thanks, once again, to top chef Derek Fuller, from whose recipe I have made this adaptation.

10 oz (275 g) cottage cheese	1 dessertspoon snipped fresh chives or spring onion tops
3 fl oz (75 ml) mayonnaise	
1 × 0.4 oz (11 g) sachet powdered gelatine (or a vegetarian alternative)	2 tablespoons cold water
	2 teaspoons lemon juice
2 oz (50 g) Sage Derby cheese	5 fl oz (150 ml) double cream
2 oz (50 g) Double Gloucester cheese with chives	Salt and freshly milled black pepper
2 oz (50 g) Blue Wensleydale cheese (note: or any other combination of cheese)	You will need a terrine or loaf tin 7 × 3½ × 2 inches (18 × 9 × 5 cm), lightly greased with groundnut oil.
½ teaspoon dillweed	

Start off by dealing with the gelatine: place it in an old teacup with 2 tablespoons cold water and 2 teaspoons lemon juice, and let it soak for about 5 minutes. Then place the cup in a saucepan containing 2 inches (5 cm) barely simmering water. Keep the heat as low as possible, and leave the gelatine to dissolve and become transparent. If you use a vegetarian alternative, follow the instructions on the packet. Meanwhile, dice the three hard cheeses into ¼ inch (5 mm) pieces and combine. Then blend the cottage cheese and the mayonnaise together until absolutely smooth. Next whip up the cream until it has thickened to the floppy stage – it should not be *too* thick.

Now in a large bowl combine the cottage-cheese mixture with the gelatine (which should be put through a strainer first). Stir the mixture really well to distribute the gelatine evenly, then add the diced cheeses, the herbs and a good seasoning of salt and pepper. Finally fold in the cream, and pour the whole lot into the terrine. (This should be done speedily or else it will begin to set.) Cover the terrine with cling film and chill for several hours till firmly set. To turn it out, carefully slide a palette knife around the edge, invert the terrine on to a serving plate and give the base a sharp tap. Serve the terrine in slices.

NOTE: If you want a larger quantity for a Christmas party, double the ingredients and use a terrine measuring 12 × 4 × 2¾ inches (30 × 10 × 7 cm).

A terrine of four cheeses (see above).

CHEESE *and* PARSNIP ROULADE *with* SAGE *and* ONION STUFFING

·

SERVES 4 PEOPLE

*T*his recipe is in specific response to the letter I received from a vegetarian last Christmas *(see the introduction on page 84). He asked if I could devise something that had stuffing, sauce and all the trimmings – so that he could feel as Christmassy as everyone else. Well, here it is, and I would add that it also goes very well with Bread sauce (see page 197) or Cranberry and orange relish (see page 193).*

FOR THE ROULADE:	3 level teaspoons dried sage
1½ oz (40 g) butter	1 tablespoon chopped fresh parsley
1 oz (25 g) plain flour	3 oz (75 g) white breadcrumbs
10 fl oz (275 ml) cold milk	Salt and freshly milled black pepper
4 oz (110 g) Sage Derby cheese, grated	
3 eggs, size 1, separated	FOR THE FILLING:
1½ oz (40 g) hazelnuts, chopped and toasted	12 oz (350 g) parsnips (prepared weight)
	1 oz (25 g) butter
1 tablespoon grated Parmesan cheese	2 tablespoons double cream
Salt and freshly milled pepper	Freshly grated nutmeg
	Salt and freshly milled black pepper
FOR THE STUFFING:	
8 oz (225 g) onions, chopped	You will need a Swiss-roll tin 13 × 9 inches
1½ oz (40 g) butter	(32 × 23 cm), lined with silicone paper.

PRE-HEAT THE OVEN TO GAS MARK 6, 400°F (200°C)

First make up the stuffing by melting the butter in a small heavy-based saucepan, then add the onions and cook them for about 6 minutes or until they are transparent. Next add the herbs, breadcrumbs and seasoning, stirring well to combine everything, then sprinkle the mixture evenly all over the silicone-lined tin.

Now for the roulade: place the butter, flour and milk in a saucepan and whisk them together over a medium heat until thickened, then season with salt and pepper and leave the sauce to cook over the gentlest possible heat for 3 minutes. After that draw the pan off the heat to cool slightly, then add the egg yolks, whisking them really well in. Next add the grated Sage Derby cheese and taste to check the seasoning.

In a large bowl (and with a spanking clean whisk) beat the egg whites until they form soft peaks. Gently fold one spoonful of the egg-white mixture into the cheese mixture – to loosen it – then spoon this mixture, a little at a time, into the rest of the egg white. Now spread the whole lot evenly into the prepared tin over the stuffing mixture, and bake on the top shelf of the oven for 20–25 minutes or until it feels springy and firm in the centre.

Meanwhile cook the parsnips in a steamer for 10–15 minutes until they're soft, then cream them together with the butter, double cream and a seasoning of nutmeg, salt and pepper (this can be done by hand or in a food processor). When they're ready, keep them warm while you lay a sheet of greaseproof paper (slightly longer than the roulade) on a work surface and sprinkle the hazelnuts all over it.

When the roulade is cooked, turn it out on to the hazelnuts and carefully peel off the base paper. Spread the creamed parsnip evenly all over the sage and onion stuffing. Then roll up the roulade along the longest side, using the greaseproof paper underneath to help you pull it into a round (it's not difficult, it behaves very well). Transfer the roulade to a serving plate and sprinkle the surface with a dusting of grated Parmesan cheese.

ROASTED RED PEPPERS STUFFED *with* FENNEL

·

SERVES 4 TO 6 PEOPLE AS A FIRST COURSE

*T*his delightful combination of flavours makes a very attractive first course. I love to serve the peppers on a faded antique plate I have, which shows off their outstanding colour. The dish needs lots of really good bread as there's always a profusion of fragrant juices.

4 large red peppers	8 dessertspoons good quality olive oil
2 small bulbs fennel	The juice of ½ lemon
1 × 14 oz (400 g) tin Italian plum tomatoes	Rock salt
1 rounded teaspoon mixed pepper berries	
¾ teaspoon whole coriander seeds	You will need a shallow baking sheet (I
½ teaspoon fennel seeds	use a Swiss-roll tin).

PRE-HEAT THE OVEN TO GAS MARK 4, 350°F (180°C)

Slice each pepper in half lengthways, cutting right through the green stalk end and leaving it intact; though it won't be eaten, it adds much to the look of the thing. Remove all the seeds. Place the pepper halves on the baking sheet, then drain the tomatoes (you don't need the juice), and divide them into eight equal portions, placing each portion inside a pepper half. Now pare off any brownish bits of fennel with your sharpest knife and cut the bulbs first into quarters and then again into eighths, carefully keeping the layers attached to the root ends. Now put them in a saucepan with a little salt, pour boiling water on them and blanch them for 5 minutes. Then drain them in a colander and, as soon as they're cool enough to handle, arrange two slices in each pepper half. Sprinkle 1 dessertspoon olive oil over each one, using a brush to brush the oil round the edges and sides of the peppers. Next lightly crush the pepper berries, coriander and fennel seeds with a pestle and mortar or rolling pin and bowl, sprinkle these evenly all over the fennel and peppers, and finish off with a grinding of rock salt. Then bake the peppers for approximately 1 hour on a high shelf in the oven until they are soft and the skin wrinkled and nicely tinged with brown. After removing them from the oven, sprinkle the lemon juice all over, cool and serve garnished with a little finely chopped spring onion or as they are.

NOTE: If you want to make the peppers ahead of time, cover with foil after cooling but don't refrigerate them as this spoils the fragrant flavour.

Roasted red peppers stuffed with fennel (see above).

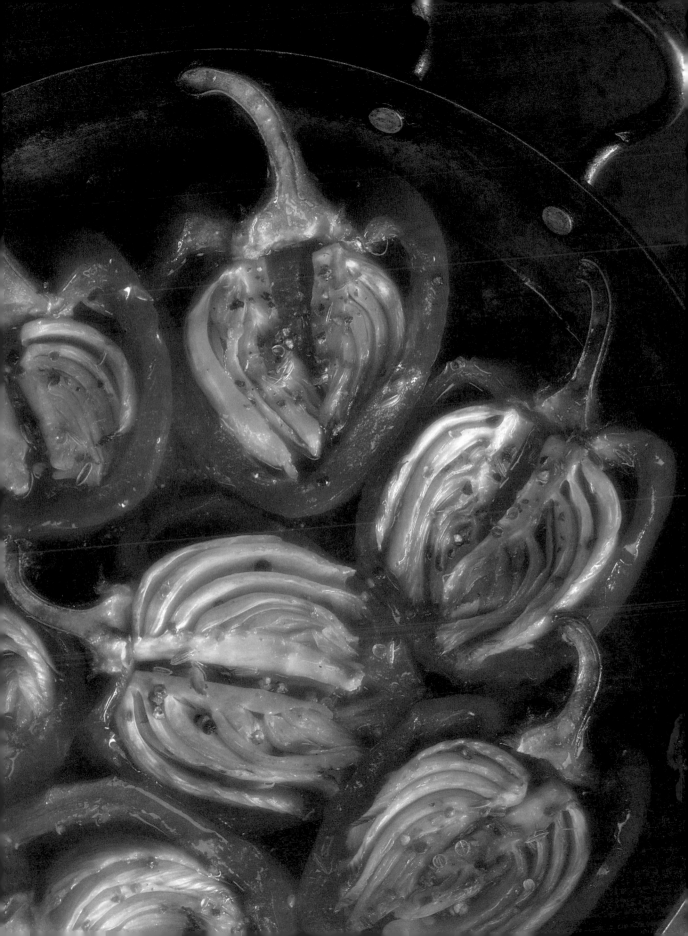

QUICK CHEESE, SAGE *and* ONION BREAD

·

SERVES 8 PEOPLE

If you wanted to serve a cold vegetarian buffet, this lovely rustic-looking loaf warm from the oven would be a perfect accompaniment. It's equally good with soup or cheese, for a snack lunch or supper.

12 oz (350 g) onions, finely chopped	4 oz (110 g) strong Cheddar cheese, grated
2 tablespoons olive oil	1 egg, size 1
12 oz (350 g) self-raising flour	Approximately 5 tablespoons milk
2 teaspoons salt	
2 teaspoons mustard powder	You will need a solid baking sheet, well greased.
24 fresh sage leaves, snipped across into thin strips	

PRE-HEAT THE OVEN TO GAS MARK 5, 375°F (190°C)

Begin by heating the oil in a large frying-pan then, keeping the heat at medium, brown the onions for 10 minutes – they need to be tender and quite well tinged with brown at the edges. Remove the pan from the heat and leave the onions to cool.

Now place the flour, onions, salt, mustard powder, grated cheese and sage strips in a large mixing bowl and mix everything evenly together. In a smaller bowl beat the egg with the milk, and add enough of this liquid to the dry ingredients to make a soft dough. Start this mixing process with a palette knife, then finish off with your hands, kneading gently until the dough is smooth.

Transfer the dough to your prepared baking sheet and roll it out gently to an 8 inch (20 cm) round. Now, using a sharp knife, make deep cuts in the top of the dough to form twelve wedges. Brush with any left-over egg and milk mixture, then bake in the centre of the oven for about 45 minutes, by which time it will be a good golden-brown colour. Serve it as fresh as possible (but it does freeze and will re-heat without any ill-effects).

◆ ● ◆

ITALIAN RISOTTO *with* WILD MUSHROOMS

·

SERVES 2 PEOPLE AS A MAIN COURSE OR 4 TO 6 AS A FIRST COURSE

This is a classic Italian, creamy-verging-on-soupy risotto which, flavoured with white wine, Parmesan cheese and dried wild porcini mushrooms, is an absolute joy for both vegetarians and non-vegetarians. You can't make this ahead of time, and since it needs close attention it should ideally be made by someone who wants to escape the chatter and have a bit of space before supper is served.

6 oz (175 g) Italian arborio rice	1 onion, finely chopped
1 pint (570 ml) boiling water	1 glass dry white wine
½ oz (15 g) packet dried porcini mushrooms (available from delicatessens or Italian shops)	2½ oz (65 g) butter
	2 tablespoons grated Parmesan cheese, plus extra to serve
8 oz (225 g) fresh mushrooms, chopped	Salt and freshly milled black pepper

Begin by placing the dried mushrooms in a bowl and pouring over the boiling water, then leave them to soak for 30 minutes while you melt 2 oz (50 g) of the butter in a large heavy-based saucepan. Add the onion and fresh mushrooms, and let these cook very, very gently until the onion is pale gold.

When the porcini have soaked, drain them (reserving the soaking water), squeeze any excess moisture from them with your hands, then chop them very small before adding them to the other mushrooms and onion. Now stir in the rice and cook for 1 or 2 minutes, stirring the grains to get them nicely coated with the buttery juices. Next pour in the wine and add a little salt and stir. Keeping the heat low, leave the rice to absorb the wine fully (about 10 minutes) – don't put a lid on.

Meanwhile bring the mushroom-soaking liquid up to the boil in a separate pan, then when the wine has been absorbed you can add a ladleful of mushroom liquid to the rice. Stir again and allow it to be gently absorbed by the rice before adding the rest – a ladleful at a time – stirring after each addition and waiting for that to be absorbed. In fact you will probably only need 15 fl oz (425 ml) of the mushroom liquid – the finished risotto should be creamy with very little visible liquid but just enough to keep it soupy rather than mushy and sticky. There is a moment when the right degree of creaminess is achieved and the grains of rice are still firm to the bite. At the end, stir in the remaining ½ oz (15 g) butter plus 2 tablespoons grated Parmesan and some seasoning. Serve the risotto with more Parmesan sprinkled on top.

CHAPTER 6

Ducks, Geese AND Game

One of the happy circumstances of celebrating the Christmas festival in mid-winter is that it coincides with the peak season not just of turkeys, but also of geese and all kinds of game. This gives us an enormous choice both for Christmas lunch itself and for all the other kinds of entertaining that will crop up.

In Britain the goose always used to be the favoured bird at the Christmas table. For centuries geese were marched from their breeding grounds in the country, on journeys that might take weeks, to the outskirts of the cities, where they would be re-fattened for market. But whereas turkeys later on submitted to being shod in tar and leather for the walk, geese stubbornly resisted the option (hence the impossibility of 'shoeing a goose'). In recent years they have returned to popularity – and at least now get transported to market!

Be that as it may, I personally feel that a goose is more appropriate for a Christmas dinner party or New Year's celebration than for Christmas lunch itself – the reason being that there is never enough left over, and I like to put my feet up on Boxing Day! However, a goose always features somewhere in my Christmas plans, not least because I would hate to miss out on that very special flavour. Ducks, too (which have never been short on flavour), do not offer rich pickings for Boxing Day, although varieties are now being bred with meatier flesh and less fat – Gressingham and Barbary ducks are good examples. But if you are only cooking Christmas lunch for two a roast duck is well worth considering.

The great virtue of game birds is that they still offer the rich 'free-range' flavour that we have almost lost in chicken: indeed, a pheasant (with all the trimmings) invariably takes me back to my childhood, recapturing what a good old roast chicken tasted like then. For a small family (of two or three) a brace of pheasant provides a real taste of luxury and – if the gluts of recent years continue – at not too exorbitant a price. Like turkey, pheasant is excellent cold the next day and makes wonderful sandwiches! Give a thought to venison at this time of the year as well. It is being much more widely farmed nowadays and so is more available than it once was: highly recommended as an unusual alternative for a party.

Game of all descriptions needs to come from a trusted supplier, who can tell you how long it has hung and the age of the bird. Old birds won't roast successfully however skilful the cooking: on the other hand, they have an infinitely better flavour than young birds when slowly braised or casseroled. And flavour is what this chapter is about – in this bland technological age let us be thankful that ducks, geese and most game birds at least have defied attempts to rear them intensively.

ROAST SEVILLE ORANGE-GLAZED DUCK *with* PORT WINE SAUCE

·

SERVES 4 PEOPLE

If you are buying marmalade for this, do try to find a good quality Seville orange variety as the bitterer flavour is important for this recipe.

1 duck with giblets, weighing approximately 5–6 lb (2.25–2.75 kg)	FOR THE SAUCE:
	1 teaspoon coriander seeds, crushed
Salt and freshly milled black pepper	1½ tablespoons lemon juice
1 bunch watercress to garnish	1 fat clove garlic, crushed
	The grated zest and juice of 1 medium orange
FOR THE GLAZE:	
1 heaped tablespoon fine-cut Seville orange marmalade, mixed with 2 tablespoons port	8 fl oz (225 ml) stock made with the duck giblets (see page 206)
	3 tablespoons port
	3 tablespoons Seville orange marmalade
	Salt and freshly milled black pepper

PRE-HEAT THE OVEN TO GAS MARK 7, 425°F (220°C)

Place the duck in a roasting tin, and prick the fleshy parts with a skewer. Season all over with salt and pepper, then roast it on the highest shelf of the oven for 20 minutes. After that reduce the heat to gas mark 4, 350°F (180°C), and continue to roast for a further 2½ hours. From time to time during the cooking remove the tin from the oven and drain off the fat into a bowl (it's wonderful for roasting potatoes). Ten minutes before the end of the cooking, brush the marmalade glaze all over the skin of the duck and return it to the oven for its final cooking. Remove the duck to a carving board to rest while you make the sauce.

Strain off all the excess fat from the roasting tin, then place the tin on a gentle heat and add the coriander seeds and garlic. Let these cook together for a minute or two as you stir and scrape off all the residue from the sides of the tin. Now pour in the stock, lemon juice and orange juice and zest, bring to simmering point, taste and season and simmer gently for 15 minutes.

During the last 5 minutes carve the duck by using a sharp knife to cut it into quarters. Arrange these on a warmed serving plate. Finally, stir the marmalade and the port into the sauce and pour it on to the duck. Garnish with watercress and serve immediately.

ROAST STUFFED GOOSE *with* PRUNES *in* ARMAGNAC

·

SERVES 8 PEOPLE

This is a supremely beautiful way of cooking and serving goose for a dinner party. It has a classic English forcemeat stuffing made with the goose liver along with pork, sage and onion, with a second spicy prune and apple stuffing, and then it's finally served with prunes that have been soaked in Armagnac. All this together makes a wonderful combination of flavours. Serve it with crunchy roast potatoes and braised red cabbage (see page 144).

1 young goose with giblets, weighing 10–12 lb (4.5–5.5 kg) oven-ready

Salt and freshly milled black pepper

A little wine for the gravy

FOR THE PRUNES IN ARMAGNAC:

12 oz (350 g) dried prunes

1 pint (570 ml) cold tea

2 oz (50 g) granulated sugar

5 fl oz (150 ml) Armagnac

FOR THE APPLE STUFFING:

1½ lb (700 g) Bramley apples, cut roughly into ½ inch (1 cm) slices

½ lb (225 g) prunes, soaked, stoned and chopped

1 large onion, roughly chopped

2 tablespoons Armagnac

⅛ teaspoon ground cloves

¼ teaspoon ground mace

Salt and freshly milled black pepper

FOR THE FORCEMEAT STUFFING:

The goose liver, finely chopped

1 Cox's apple, finely chopped

10 oz (275 g) minced pork or good quality pork sausagemeat

1 medium onion, finely chopped

2 oz (50 g) breadcrumbs

2 level teaspoons dried sage

Salt and freshly milled black pepper

PRE-HEAT THE OVEN TO GAS MARK 7, 425°F (220°C)

You can prepare the prunes several days in advance. Soak them overnight in the cold tea, then drain them, barely cover with water, add the sugar and simmer for 15 minutes. Drain, sprinkle over the Armagnac, cover and leave in the refrigerator.

Make the apple stuffing by mixing all the ingredients together and make the forcemeat stuffing, too, by mixing all the ingredients together.

When you are ready to cook the goose, begin by placing the forcemeat stuffing into the neck flap end of the bird, pressing it in as far as you can, tucking the

Pheasants hanging outside R. Allen's shop in London.

neck flap all round it and patting it with your hands to make a rounded shape. Secure the flap underneath with a small skewer. Next, place the apple stuffing in the body cavity as it is – although it looks raw and chunky, after cooking it will collapse to a fluffy mass.

Season the goose well with salt and pepper, lay in on a rack in a roasting tin, then place it in the centre of the pre-heated oven. Give it 30 minutes' initial cooking, then reduce the temperature to gas mark 4, 350°F (180°C), and roast another 3 hours. That is for an 11 lb (5 kg) goose plus stuffing; allow 15 minutes less for a 10 lb (4.5 kg) bird, 15 minutes more for a 12 lb (5.5 kg) one.

Make a stock with the giblets (see page 206).

When the goose is cooked the juices will run clear when you pierce the thickest part of the leg with a skewer. Remove the bird to a serving dish, snap off the wing tips and allow to rest for 20 minutes or so before serving.

Now drain off the fat from the tin and make a light gravy from the remaining residue, the giblet stock and a little wine. Then heat the prunes gently in a frying-pan and transfer them to a warmed serving dish. After carving the goose give each person a little of each of the stuffings, and serve the gravy and sauce separately.

ROAST GOOSE *with* POTATO, SAGE *and* APPLE STUFFING *served with* SPICED PICKLED PEARS

·

SERVES 8 PEOPLE

Here is another superb way to serve goose. If you haven't made the Spiced pickled pears well in advance (see page 57), fear not – they are almost as good served straightaway as when they have had a chance to mature.

1 young goose with giblets, weighing 10–12 lb (4.5–5.5 kg) oven-ready	2 medium Bramley apples, peeled and chopped
	1 tablespoon chopped parsley
FOR THE STUFFING:	1 tablespoon chopped sage leaves
1½ lb (700 g) red potatoes	2 oz (50 g) butter
8 oz (225 g) onions, finely chopped	Salt and freshly milled black pepper

PRE-HEAT THE OVEN TO GAS MARK 7, 425°F (220°C)

Begin by peeling the potatoes and chopping them into ¾ inch (2 cm) cubes. Place them in a saucepan with some salt, then cover them with boiling water and simmer for about 8 minutes or until they're just tender. Meanwhile melt the butter in a large frying-pan and cook the onions and apples gently for about 10 minutes, then add the sage and parsley and finally the drained potatoes. Stir to mix everything thoroughly, season with salt and pepper, then pack the stuffing into the body cavity of the goose.

Roast the bird in exactly the same way as on page 107. Serve with a gravy made from goose giblet stock (see page 206) and the roasting-tin juices remaining after the fat has been drained off. Give each person some of the stuffing and have a bowl of Spiced pickled pears, reheated for 5 minutes in their own juices, on the table for everyone to help themselves. (I have one very enthusiastic friend who managed no less than four pickled pears at one sitting!)

◆ ● ◆

PHEASANT ROASTED *in* BUTTER MUSLIN *served with* CRANBERRY *and* ONION CONFIT

·

SERVES 4 TO 6 PEOPLE

*I*f *you want to roast pheasants that are guaranteed to be moist and tender, then this is the best way I've come across. Do remember, though, to check with your supplier that the pheasants are young enough to roast. Older birds should always be braised or casseroled (see page 112).*

	FOR THE GRAVY:
1 brace pheasants weighing about 1½ lb (700 g) each	Stock made with the pheasant giblets (see page 206)
4 rashers unsmoked streaky bacon	2 tablespoons port or Madeira
4 oz (110 g) butter	1 teaspoon redcurrant jelly
A few sprigs fresh thyme	A little plain flour
2 bayleaves, snipped into 4 pieces	Salt and freshly milled black pepper
Salt and freshly milled black pepper	

You will need 2 pieces of muslin 18 × 18 inches (45 × 45 cm) and some wooden cocktail sticks.

PRE-HEAT THE OVEN TO GAS MARK 8, 450°F (230°C)

Wipe the birds with some kitchen paper and trim off any odd bits of skin that are hanging loose. Then, beginning at the neck cavity of each bird, pinch the skin to loosen it and provide a kind of pocket along each side of the breast. Next insert the pieces of bacon, snipping them in half if you need to, so that what you end up with is breast covered by bacon covered by skin. Now place each bird in the centre of a piece of muslin, season with salt and freshly milled black pepper and plaster each pheasant with butter spread thickly all over. Wrap the muslin up like a parcel, bringing the first two opposite edges up, one over the other, then tuck the thyme and bayleaves in and finally fold the other two edges over and secure the parcels at both ends with cocktail sticks.

Now place the birds in a roasting tin on a high shelf in the oven and give them 30 minutes, then reduce the heat to gas mark 5, 375°F (190°C), and continue to cook the pheasants for a further hour, basting with the butter from time to time. When a pheasant thigh is pierced with a skewer and the juices run clear it's done. Discard the muslin and leave the birds to rest in a warm place whilst you make a gravy. Spoon off all the excess fat from the roasting tin, and place the tin over a medium heat. Stir in a little flour till smooth, then gradually add enough stock to make a thinnish sauce. Season with salt and freshly milled black pepper and let the gravy bubble and reduce before stirring in the redcurrant jelly and the port or Madeira. Serve the pheasant with the gravy and Cranberry and onion confit handed round separately.

NOTE: One pheasant cooked in this way with the Cranberry and onion confit would make a wonderful Christmas lunch for two people.

CRANBERRY *and* ONION CONFIT

A confit, as the name suggests, is a kind of sauce reduced to a concentrated jam-like consistency. The quantity below will probably be twice as much as you need for the roast pheasants, but I suggest you make the full amount as it is such a good accompaniment for all kinds of things at Christmas. As it keeps well in the refrigerator for 4 weeks, I personally make double the quantity below and serve it with cold turkey, pheasant, pork pies or, perhaps best of all, with sausages. In fact venison sausages with Cranberry and onion confit, creamed mashed potatoes and braised red cabbage is a very princely meal fit for any Christmas supper party.

1 lb (450 g) onions, peeled and chopped smallish but not minute	4 oz (110 g) cranberries
1 clove garlic, crushed	The grated zest and juice of ½ large or 1 small orange
1 oz (25 g) granulated sugar	¼ teaspoon cardamom seeds, crushed
1 oz (25 g) butter	Salt and freshly milled black pepper
2½ fl oz (65 ml) red wine vinegar	

In a saucepan melt the butter over a gentle heat and stir in the onions, garlic and sugar. Then, keeping the heat very low, allow them to cook slowly for about 15 minutes, giving them quite frequent stirs to keep them on the move and allow them to colour evenly. After that add all the rest of the ingredients, stir well and then cover the pan. Cook gently for another 10–15 minutes or until all the cranberries have burst. Then remove the lid and continue to cook gently for about 40 minutes or until you have a reduced, thickened, almost paste-like consistency. Allow it to get completely cold, spoon it into a poly-thene container, cover and chill in the refrigerator till needed. The flavour will be best if you bring it back to room temperature before serving.

111

BRAISED PHEASANTS *in* MADEIRA

·

SERVES 4 TO 6 PEOPLE

Because older birds are not tender enough to be roasted they are excellent slowly braised and tenderised in a beautiful sauce (see page 114). The advantage of a little age is, of course, a lot more flavour, so this is probably one of the nicest pheasant dishes of all. It also improves if you make it the day before you need it and re-heat gently before serving. The recipe is suitable for freezing.

1 brace pheasants, oven-ready	2 bayleaves
10 fl oz (275 ml) stock made with the pheasant giblets (see page 206)	8 oz (225 g) small open-cap mushrooms
	10 fl oz (275 ml) dry white wine
1½ oz (40 g) butter	10 fl oz (275 ml) Sercial Madeira
1½ tablespoons groundnut oil	1½ oz (40 g) butter, softened
12 oz (350 g) streaky bacon (in one piece if you can get it)	1½ oz (40 g) plain flour
	Salt and freshly milled black pepper
16 pink shallots, peeled	
2 cloves garlic, finely chopped	You will need a large shallow flameproof
5 sprigs fresh thyme	casserole.

If you haven't managed to persuade your supplier to do it for you, begin by jointing the pheasants. This you do with your very sharpest knife as follows: hold the pheasant with the breastbone uppermost, make a small incision at the back end, then turn the pheasant up, neck end down, in a vertical position, insert the knife where you made your cut and cut right down to the neck end. Then open the bird out flat, skin side down, and cut all along the backbone. Now turn each side skin side up and pull each end, stretching the whole thing out as far as you can. This will reveal a line which naturally separates the two joints, so simply cut along this line. Do the same with the other half and you will have four joints.

Begin cooking the joints of pheasant by seasoning them with salt and pepper and frying them in butter and oil until they have taken on a good golden-brown colour. As they brown transfer them to the casserole. Then, in the fat remaining in the pan, fry the shallots until golden-brown and also remove them with a slotted spoon to a plate. The bacon should be rinded and cut into ⅓ inch (7.5 mm) cubes and browned as well. Then remove these to join the shallots and leave aside for later.

Now add the thyme, bayleaves and chopped garlic to the pheasant and pour in the stock, wine and Madeira. Bring everything to simmering point, then keep the heat low so that the contents just gently, almost imperceptibly bubble. Put on a tight-fitting lid and cook on top of the stove for 45 minutes. After that add the small whole mushrooms, the bacon and shallots, and spoon some of the juices over them. Then put the lid on, bring everything back to a gentle simmer and simmer for a further 45 minutes or until the pheasant is tender when tested with a small skewer.

To finish the sauce, mix the softened butter and flour to a smooth paste. Then, using a slotted spoon, remove the pheasant, bacon and vegetables from the casserole to a warmed serving dish and keep warm. Bring the liquid up to a fast boil and let it bubble and reduce by about one-third. Next add the butter and flour mixture, using a wire whisk to distribute it. Then, as soon as the sauce comes back to the boil and has thickened, pour it over the pheasant, bacon and vegetables and serve; or cool, refrigerate and re-heat gently the next day.

Although imported new potatoes are not very flavoursome in the winter months they are an ideal accompaniment to something very flavoursome like this and a few snipped chives sprinkled on them improve their flavour. A little steamed broccoli or tiny button sprouts would also be a good accompaniment.

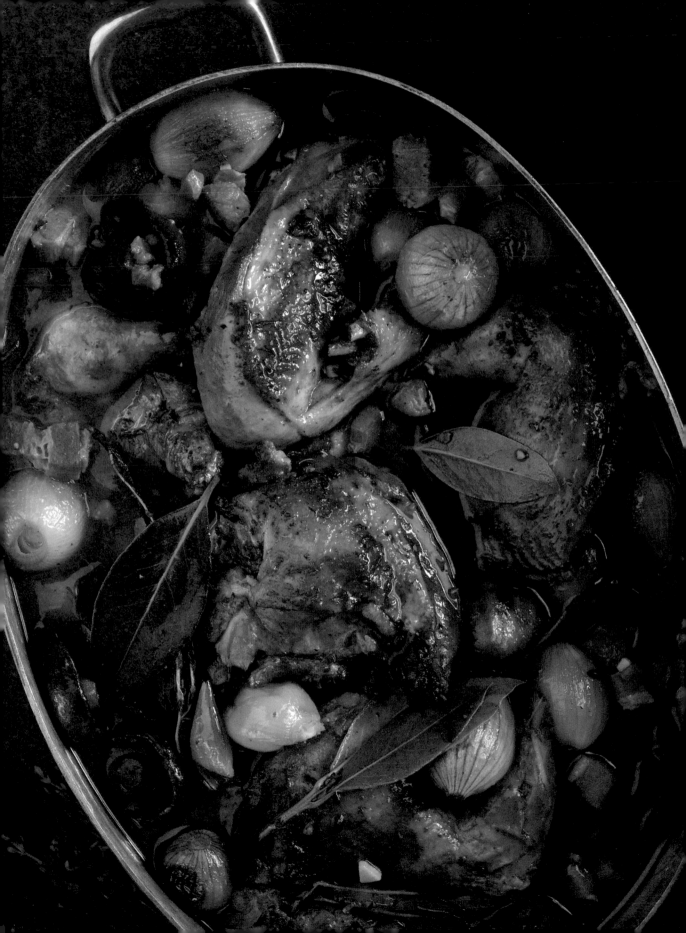

VENISON *(or beef)* with PORT, GUINNESS *and* PICKLED WALNUTS

·

SERVES 10 TO 12 PEOPLE

T*his is a very special braised dish that is wonderful for a party since it demands no last-minute attention or fuss. You can use shoulder of venison – which will give a richer, more gamy flavour – or a well flavoured cut of beef such as brisket. Serve with Traditional braised red cabbage and Purée of potato and celeriac with garlic (see pages 144 and 141).*

6 lb (2.75 kg) venison or beef, cut into 1 inch (2.5 cm) squares	2 cloves garlic, crushed
2 pints (1.2 litres) Guinness	2 × 14 oz (400 g) jars pickled walnuts
10 fl oz (275 ml) port	3 tablespoons butter
2 bayleaves	3 tablespoons olive oil
4 sprigs thyme	2 level tablespoons flour
8 oz (225 g) onions, chopped	Salt and freshly milled black pepper

Begin this the night before by placing the meat in a large bowl along with the bayleaves and thyme. Pour the Guinness and port all over it, place a plate on top of the meat (to keep it pushed down into the marinade as much as possible), and leave in a cool place overnight. The next day, stir everything well.

When you're ready to cook the meat, pre-heat the oven to gas mark 1, 275°F (140°C). Take a large flameproof casserole, add half the butter and oil to it and heat gently. Drain the meat (reserving the liquid and herbs), and dry a few pieces at a time with kitchen paper. Turn the heat up high, then add these few pieces to the pan to brown them (if you add too much meat in one go, it will release too much steam and not brown sufficiently). As soon as they're browned, remove them and continue until all the meat is browned.

Now add the rest of the butter and oil to the pan and as soon as it foams and bubbles add the chopped onions and garlic to brown these for about 10 minutes. Meanwhile drain all the liquid off the walnuts and cut them into quarters. Return all the meat to the casserole to join the onions. Stir in the flour to soak up all the juices, then pour in the marinade (including the bayleaves and thyme), add the walnut quarters, and season well with salt and pepper.

As soon as it reaches a gentle simmer, put a lid on, transfer the casserole to the middle shelf of the oven and forget all about it for 3 hours – by which time the meat will be tender and the sauce marvellously dark and rich.

Braised pheasants in Madeira (see page 112).

OLD-FASHIONED RAISED GAME PIE

·

SERVES 12 PEOPLE

This recipe is not quite as difficult as it might seem from the daunting lists below. Once you have assembled and sorted out all the ingredients you are well on your way. It can be made a day or two before you need to serve it, and it's excellent for a cold buffet (see page 118), served in slices with Cumberland sauce (see page 129) or Cranberry and onion confit (see page 111).

FOR THE JELLIED STOCK:
All the bones and scraps from the game

4 allspice berries

1 blade mace

6 whole black peppercorns

1 level teaspoon dried thyme

2 bayleaves

1 carrot

1 onion, stuck with 4 cloves

Lemon juice

1 × 0.4 oz (11 g) sachet powdered gelatine

Salt

FOR THE FILLING:
1½ lb (700 g) haunch or saddle of venison

1 small hare, jointed

(or any other combination of game,

provided you finish up with 2 lb (1 kg)

game meat after trimming)

5 fl oz (150 ml) tawny port

2 tablespoons brandy

½ teaspoon dried thyme

1 lb (450 g) hard back pork fat

1 lb (450 g) lean pork

1¼ teaspoons ground ginger

1¼ teaspoons ground cinnamon

¾ teaspoon freshly grated nutmeg

1 clove garlic, crushed

2–3 tablespoons fresh chopped parsley

8 oz (225 g) thin green back bacon rashers

Salt and freshly milled black pepper

FOR THE HOT-WATER CRUST PASTRY:
1¼ lb (560 g) plain flour

¾ teaspoon salt

1 tablespoon icing sugar

¼ teaspoon ground mace

7 oz (200 g) lard

8 fl oz (250 ml) water

Beaten egg to glaze

You will need an 8 inch (20 cm) round
cake tin with a removable base.

Stage one starts off the day before you make the pie itself. First trim all the game meat from the bones and cut it into ¼–½ inch (5 mm–1 cm) cubes. Any really scrappy pieces can be saved for mincing together with the pork the next day, and any sinewy bits can go in the stock. Place the cubed meat in a bowl, pour in the port and brandy, sprinkle with the thyme, salt and pepper, then stir well, cover and leave in a cool place to marinate overnight.

Next place the game bones (plus bits) in a deep saucepan with enough cold water to cover. Add the spices and herbs for the jellied stock, together with the carrot and onion stuck with cloves (but don't add any salt). Bring to the boil and simmer gently for about 2 hours – you will need to skim the surface of the stock during the initial stages of the cooking. After that strain the stock into a fresh saucepan, discard all the debris and boil rapidly until it has reduced to about 1 pint (570 ml) and has a good flavour. Taste and season with salt and lemon juice as required, then whisk in the gelatine. Cover the mixture and chill overnight.

Stage two takes place the following day. Make sure the jellied stock has set and skim the surface thoroughly. Now butter your cake tin and pre-heat the oven to gas mark 2, 300°F (150°C). Next finely mince together the pork fat, lean pork and any game scraps from the day before. Add the spices, garlic, parsley and a seasoning of salt and pepper: mix this thoroughly, then divide the mixture into four. Shape each quarter into a flat round slightly smaller than the diameter of the cake tin (wet your hands for this job to make it easier).

Now for the pastry: prepare the hot-water crust by sifting all the dry ingredients together in a bowl. Place the lard and 8 fl oz (250 ml) water in a saucepan and heat until the lard has melted and the water is boiling. Then immediately pour the liquid into the dry ingredients and stir with a spoon to form a dough. Turn the dough out on to a working surface and knead very lightly and briefly.

Now weigh 1 lb 5 oz (600 g) of the dough, put it in a loosely folded plastic bag and let it cool a little before rolling it out to a round similar in diameter to that of the cake tin. Place the round of dough in the tin, then gradually work it from the centre of the base and up the sides of the tin. Work your way round the tin, using your curled-up fingers as a pad, gently squeezing the dough up the side and just over the rim. Make sure the pastry is as even as possible with no obvious cracks or thin places.

Next line the inside of the pastry mould with the bacon rashers, cutting them level with the top of the tin. Place a round of the pork mixture in the base and pat it out to fit the interior. Now cover that with a third of the marinated game and its juices. Repeat this layering twice more and finish off with a pork mixture layer. Roll out the rest of the dough to a round suitable for a lid, glaze the inside of the dough with egg and press into position on top of the pie. Squeeze the edges together and trim down with scissors to give an edge of about ½ inch (1 cm) standing up proud. Next turn the edge firmly over inwards, pressing it down with the prongs of a fork. Make a steam hole in the top, then re-roll the pastry trimmings and cut out diamond-shaped leaves to decorate the lid.

Now lay a sheet of foil over the top and bake for 2½ hours, then remove from the oven. Leave the pie for 30–45 minutes to firm up, then turn up the oven temperature to gas mark 5, 375°F (190°C). Carefully remove the pie from the tin and brush the pastry all over with egg. (If the sides show any sign of bulging,

117

encircle the pie with a band of greaseproof paper and tie with string.) Return the pie to the oven and as the pastry continues baking it will firm up (if you used the paper, you will gradually be able to peel it away, but add a little more egg to the unglazed parts) and all the pastry will brown – it will take approximately 30 minutes. As the top will brown before the sides, it will need to be protected with foil while the sides finish browning.

When the pie is a glowing golden colour remove from the oven, leave to cool, then cover and chill. Meanwhile have the jellied stock warmed slightly (by sitting it in a bowl of hot water), then cool it to the syrupy stage and pour it into the pie very gradually via the steam hole (as much as it will take). Chill again to give the jelly a chance to set and then – believe it or not – it's ready to serve.

For a Raised Pork Pie

For a variation on the Old-fashioned raised game pie recipe you can make a Raised pork pie. You will need:

3 lb (1.5 kg) pork shoulder, coarsely minced or chopped small	12 oz (350 g) pork back fat, coarsely minced or chopped small
Some pork bones	

All other ingredients, the method and timings are as above.

Old-fashioned raised game pie (see page 116) and Pheasant terrine (see page 120).

PHEASANT TERRINE

·

SERVES 10 TO 12 PEOPLE

This is excellent served as a light lunch with lovely crisp gherkins and lightly toasted bread (see page 118). It also goes a long way at a help-yourself buffet party, or as a first course with some Cranberry and onion confit (see page 111) – but don't be tempted to serve too big portions as a first course because it is very rich.

1 plump young hen pheasant, plucked and dressed	2 cloves garlic, crushed
12 oz (350 g) lean veal, minced	1 teaspoon mixed pepper berries (see page 56), crushed
1 lb (450 g) fat belly of pork, minced	15 juniper berries, crushed
8 oz (225 g) turkey livers, minced	5 fl oz (150 ml) dry white wine
10 oz (275 g) unsmoked lean bacon, chopped small	1 fl oz (25 ml) brandy
1 rounded teaspoon salt	You will need a 3 pint (1.75 litre) loaf tin or terrine.
½ teaspoon mace	

Begin by removing all the meat from the pheasant. The best way of going about this is as if you were boning it: that is, start by turning the bird breast side down and cutting down the length of the backbone. With a small sharp knife work your way down one side of the bird, severing the legs and wings from the body as you work down to them, and on until the top edge of the breastbone is reached. Do the same with the other side, then lift the carcase from the skin and meat. Remove the meat from the skin; cut the meat from the leg and wing joints, then cut the larger pieces of meat into sugar cube-sized pieces, discarding any remaining skin, sinew or shot (all the discarded bits, including the carcase could be used to make some stock to store in the freezer).

To make the terrine, mix the pheasant meat thoroughly with all the other ingredients. Cover and leave in a cool place for several hours.

Then, before cooking the terrine, pre-heat the oven to gas mark 2, 300°F (150°C). Stir everything in the bowl again, then press the mixture into the terrine and place that in a meat roasting tin half filled with hot water. Bake the terrine for about 1¾–2 hours – by the time it has cooked it will have shrunk quite a bit from the sides of the tin. Remove from the oven and leave to cool without draining off any of the juices because when cold the surrounding fat will help to keep the terrine moist, even though you won't actually eat any of it.

When the terrine is cold place a double sheet of foil over it and put some scale weights on top to press it down for a few hours: this is not essential but helps to make the terrine less crumbly if you want to serve it in neat slices.

POT-ROASTED PARTRIDGES *with* JUNIPER STUFFING

·

SERVES 4 PEOPLE

This is a recipe which I've adapted from one given me by Susan Constantine-Smith, who founded and runs the Suffolk Larder (see page 219) with her husband, Tony. I like to serve this with some plain boiled cabbage.

2 plump young partridges, plucked and dressed	FOR THE STUFFING:
4 rashers streaky bacon	4 oz (110 g) smoked bacon, finely chopped
15 fl oz (425 ml) dry white wine or cider	1 tablespoon olive oil
2 tablespoons olive oil	1 tablespoon chopped fresh parsley
4 shallots, chopped	1 level teaspoon chopped fresh thyme
1 medium carrot, sliced	1 tablespoon juniper berries, crushed
1 Cox's apple	2 tablespoons white wine
The grated zest of ½ lemon	2 slices white bread, trimmed and cut into small cubes
Salt and freshly milled black pepper	Salt and freshly milled black pepper
Chopped parsley to garnish	

PRE-HEAT THE OVEN TO GAS MARK 4, 350°F (180°C)

First make the stuffing by heating 1 tablespoon oil in a heavy frying-pan and frying the finely chopped bacon till crisp. Use a draining spoon to transfer it to a bowl and then mix it thoroughly with all the other stuffing ingredients. Season well, then pack the stuffing inside the body cavity of each bird.

Now heat 2 more tablespoons oil in the same frying-pan, and while that's happening drape the bacon slices over the birds lengthways, then tie the birds in a couple of places widthways to hold the bacon in place. Next brown the birds, bacon and all, in the hot oil before transferring them both to a medium-sized flameproof casserole. Add the shallots and carrot, tucking them around the birds. Quarter and core the apple and then grate it straight into the casserole all around the partridges. Now add the lemon zest, pour in the wine or cider, season with salt and pepper and bring the liquid up to simmering point.

Cover the casserole and transfer it to the oven to cook for 40 minutes. After that remove the lid and finish cooking (basting from time to time) for a further 10–20 minutes or until the birds are tender. Serve sprinkled with parsley.

NOTE: If you find partridges hard to come by or if you would like to make this recipe at some other time of year, it works extremely well with small poussins.

CHAPTER 7

Roasted Meats
AND
Cold Cuts

*S*o often during the rest of the year it can seem a bit extravagant to splash out on the right-sized joint of meat for roasting, but it is one of the gloriously indulgent aspects of Christmas that we can for once justify the expense of a large sirloin of beef, or a loin of pork, or even a whole ham.

I am really quite happy to eat *less* meat (for all the right economic and humane reasons), but what I am passionate about is making sure that when we do eat it it should be right; that is to say, properly reared and butchered and matured in the old-fashioned way. If this has not been done the meat will – and sadly often does – lack any flavour at all. I am also convinced that meat cooked on the bone has a succulence and flavour that no other cuts can match, which is why this chapter includes cooking instructions for the large bone-in cuts. I have not included lamb here because, quite frankly, it is not at its best in most parts of the country at this season.

What this all amounts to is, order your meat from a reliable butcher, and in good time. If you buy it from a supermarket don't forget that at the better quality retailers there is a butcher's department behind the scenes, which will be quite happy to prepare your Christmas joint to your own specifications.

COLD PRESSED OX TONGUE

·

SERVES 10 TO 12 PEOPLE

Although you can order a pressed tongue from the butcher at Christmas it is usually much nicer homemade – and it's not really much trouble. Once cooked and pressed, it's wonderful served in slices with pickles and salads, or put into sandwiches with some sharp mustard.

1 pickled ox tongue, weighing approximately 4–4½ lb (1.75–2 kg)	6 whole black peppercorns
1 large onion, quartered	6–7 pints (3.5–4 litres) cold water
2 leeks, split and washed	2 teaspoons powdered gelatine
2 carrots, cut into chunks	2 tablespoons port
1 clove garlic, peeled	
A few parsley stalks	You will need a 5–6 inch (13–15 cm) deep cake tin or soufflé dish.
1 bayleaf	

First the tongue needs to be well scrubbed with a stiff brush, then covered with cold water and left to soak for half a day or so. After that discard the water, place the tongue in a deep pan and cover with 6–7 pints (3.5–4 litres) of fresh cold water. Bring this up to the boil, then skim off all the surface scum before adding the prepared vegetables, garlic, herbs and peppercorns. Simmer very gently for about 3½ hours.

The tongue will be ready when the skin is 'blistered' and the T-shaped bone at the root comes away easily when pulled. Remove the tongue from the pan and douse it with cold water to cool, then strip away all the skin. Neaten the tongue by trimming away the ragged and gristly bits at the root and underneath, then curl it round to fit into the tin or dish.

Boil the liquor briskly to reduce it and concentrate the flavour. Now sprinkle the gelatine into a little cold water in a cup and melt it over simmering water until absolutely clear. Now strain off 10 fl oz (275 ml) of the cooking liquor, strain the gelatine into it and lastly add the port. Pour the mixture over the tongue. Place a saucer on top, weight it down heavily and leave for several hours (or overnight) until cold and set. Serve the tongue with some chopped jelly as a garnish.

◆━◆━◆

TRADITIONAL BAKED *and* GLAZED WHOLE HAM

·

SERVES 20 TO 25 PEOPLE

If you are having a houseful of people at Christmas, perhaps it is the one time of the year when a whole ham is absolutely justified. The flavour of a traditional ham is always far superior when the ham is cooked on the bone, and the bone itself will yield a wonderful stock for soup.

1 whole ham, weighing 12–14 lb (5.5–6.5 kg), pre-soaked according to supplier's instructions (see opposite)	3 heaped tablespoons demerara sugar
	About 24 whole cloves
3 heaped tablespoons prepared English mustard	You will need 2 large pieces extra-width foil and a large roasting tin.

PRE-HEAT THE OVEN TO GAS MARK 3, 325°F (160°C)

Begin by placing one sheet of foil lengthways in the roasting tin and the other piece widthways. Now remove the ham from the soaking water and place it in the middle of the foil, then bring the widthways piece of foil up to the centre and fold the edges over twice to weld them together. The ham needs air to circulate round it during the cooking, so the less the foil actually touches it the better. Now bring the lengthways piece of foil to join the rest, and fold the edges over all round. The ham should now be sitting in a sort of tent of foil.

Next place the tin in the oven and bake it for 20 minutes per lb (450 g). That would be 4 hours for a 12 lb (5.5 kg) ham or 4 hours 40 minutes for a 14 lb (6.5 kg). Calculate when the last 30 minutes' cooking time will be, and at that point remove it from the oven (this last 30 minutes will be for the glazing). Turn the heat right up to gas mark 7, 425°F (220°C). Now open the foil and get someone to help you move the ham on to a work surface. Next, using a tea-cloth to protect your hands, take a sharp knife and make three or four horizontal incisions in the skin. Then, with the help of a knife and your protected hand, carefully remove the brown skin in strips, leaving as much fat behind as you can. To score the fat simply make cuts crossways and lengthways with the knife, forming a diamond pattern, then stud a clove into the centre of each diamond shape. Now quickly spread the mustard all over with the help of a palette knife and then finally press the sugar all over, using your hands.

Now discard the cooking foil and pour the juices in the roasting tin into a bowl to reserve them. Then place the ham back in the roasting tin and return it to the oven for a further 30 minutes or until the surface has a glazed golden crust.

If the ham is going to be served hot allow it to rest for 45 minutes after removing it from the oven so that the surface juices will seep back into the meat and the meat will firm up and be easier to carve.

If it's to be served cold simply leave it in the coolest place possible overnight.

IMPORTANT NOTE: All the precious reserved juices from the ham can be chilled in the refrigerator, the fat removed and the juices then used for enriching post-Christmas soups made with split peas, lentils or chick peas, or especially the Chestnut soup with bacon and thyme croûtons (see page 212).

Baked Glazed Boned Gammon

If a whole ham is too much, either a half ham or a large piece of boned gammon (middle-cut or corner) could be cooked in exactly the same way, following all the instructions above except that you'll need less foil and half the amount of glazing ingredients and you calculate the cooking time at 30 minutes per lb (450 g) at the same temperature. A 5–6 lb (2.25–2.75 kg) piece of rolled gammon will serve 8–10 people.

Notes on Soaking Ham

It is imperative that, before you embark on cooking any kind of whole ham, you check with the supplier the precise details of what soaking is required. The amount of soaking will depend on the quantity of salt used in the curing, and only the supplier can give this information.

A large plastic bucket seems to be the most suitable container for soaking a ham – although I have also used a picnic cool box quite successfully. Cover the ham completely with cold water and leave for as many hours as the supplier recommends. Smaller joints can be placed in a cooking pot, covered with cold water, brought up to simmering point, then the water thrown out (if you're in any doubt about the saltiness, taste a sliver of the meat to make sure).

ROAST LOIN *of* PORK *with* HERBS *and* SPICED APRICOTS

·

SERVES 8 PEOPLE

This Christmas recipe for pork uses the loin, which yields lots of crunchy crackling, roasted with aromatic herbs. It is served with a sweet and sour sauce made with our Spiced apricot and orange chutney (see page 60) simmered with some sweetish white wine such as Riesling. Crisp roast potatoes and Traditional braised red cabbage with apples (see page 144) make a wonderful accompaniment for this.

1 loin of pork, weighing approximately 4 lb (1.75 kg), with the skin scored	FOR THE SAUCE:
	The pork pan juices
3 or 4 cloves garlic, cut into slivers	½ oz (15 g) plain flour
Some tiny sprigs rosemary	1 pint (570 ml) Riesling
Some tiny sprigs thyme	3 tablespoons Spiced apricot and orange
½ small onion	chutney (see page 60)
1 tablespoon rock salt	The grated zest of ½ orange
Freshly milled black pepper	Salt and freshly milled black pepper

PRE-HEAT THE OVEN TO GAS MARK 9, 475°F (240°C)

When you buy a piece of pork always look out for a dry skin – the drier the skin, the better the crackling will be. If it does look at all damp, dry it as much as possible with a cloth and leave it uncovered in the refrigerator till needed.

When you are ready to cook the pork, place it on a board and tuck little sprigs of rosemary and thyme in between the scored fat. Make little slits all over the joint with the tip of a knife (particularly near the bone) and insert the slivers of garlic in them – and a few herbs here and there as well. Now rub the surface of the skin all over with coarse rock salt and a sprinkling of pepper: this will help to give crunch to the crackling. Place the joint in a roasting tin, slipping half an onion underneath to give a good colour and flavour to the sauce in due course. Don't add any fat at all, as there is more than enough in the pork. Roast on the highest shelf in the oven for 20 minutes, then reduce the heat to gas mark 5, 375°F (190°C), and continue to cook for a further 1¾–2 hours.

When the pork is cooked, remove it to a warmed plate and keep warm. To make the sauce, discard the onion and spoon off all but 1 tablespoon fat from the roasting tin. Then sprinkle in the flour and mix to a smooth paste. Place the tin over a gentle heat and, using a wire whisk, gradually whisk in the wine, little by little, until you have a smooth sauce. Let it bubble and reduce for a few minutes, taste to check the seasoning, then finally stir in the chutney and orange zest. Simmer for about 5 minutes, then pour the sauce into a jug to hand round separately with the meat.

NOTE: If you do not have an apricot chutney, then I suggest serving this with a classic apple sauce and some Prunes in Armagnac (see page 107).

—◆—●—◆—

CUMBERLAND SAUCE

·

SERVES 8 PEOPLE

This is, for me, one of the great classic English sauces, provided it's made with a good quality redcurrant jelly with a high fruit content; some of the commercial varieties are lacking in fruit and too sickly sweet. Cumberland sauce is always served cold and is a wonderful accompaniment to either hot or cold gammon, tongue, cold goose or game and it goes extremely well with a slice of the Old-fashioned raised game pie or Pheasant terrine (see pages 116 and 120).

1 medium lemon	4 tablespoons port
1 medium orange	1 heaped teaspoon mustard powder
4 large tablespoons authentic redcurrant jelly	1 heaped teaspoon ground ginger

First, thinly pare off the rinds of both the lemon and the orange (either with a very sharp paring knife or a potato peeler), then cut them into very small strips, about ½ inch (1 cm) in length and as thin as possible. Boil the rinds in water for 5 minutes to extract any bitterness, then drain well.

Now place the redcurrant jelly in a saucepan with the port and melt, whisking them together over a low heat for about 5 or 10 minutes. The redcurrant jelly won't melt completely, so it's best to sieve it afterwards to get rid of any obstinate little globules.

In a serving bowl mix the mustard and ginger with the juice of half the lemon till smooth, then add the juice of the whole orange, the port and redcurrant mixture and finally the strips of orange and lemon peel. Mix well – and it's ready for use. Cumberland sauce stores well in a screw-top jar in the refrigerator for up to 2 weeks.

NOTE: This sauce should not be thickened – it is meant to have a thinnish consistency.

—◆—●—◆—

TRADITIONAL ROAST SIRLOIN *of* BEEF *served with* YORKSHIRE PUDDING

·

SERVES 8 PEOPLE

The only way to enjoy this most splendid of feasts is to make absolutely sure the beef is good, because in this case more than in any other the cook is at the mercy of his or her supplier. Use a known reliable butcher, a supermarket that specialises in matured traditional beef, or else a recommended mail-order supplier (see page 218). As with a whole ham, beef cooked on the bone has the best flavour of all.

1 sirloin of beef on the bone, weighing 5–6 lb (2.25–2.75 kg) – this would be 3 ribs	1 level dessertspoon mustard powder
1 level dessertspoon plain flour	½ onion, peeled
	Freshly milled black pepper

PRE-HEAT THE OVEN TO GAS MARK 9, 475°F (240°C)

Place the beef, just as it is, upright in a roasting tin, then tuck in the half onion alongside it. Combine the mustard powder and flour, then dust this all over the surface of the fat, and finally season with a few twists of freshly milled pepper. This floury surface will help to make the fat very crusty (for those like me who want to eat what I call the 'crispies'), while the onion will caramelise to give the gravy a rich colour and flavour. Place the joint in the oven – it will have plenty of fat so don't add extra. After 20 minutes turn the heat down to gas mark 5, 375°F (190°C), and continue to cook for 15 minutes per lb (450 g) for rare, plus 15 minutes extra for medium-rare or 30 minutes extra for well-done. While cooking baste the meat with the juices at least three times. To see if the beef is cooked to your liking insert a thin skewer and press out some juices: the red, pink or clear colour will indicate to what stage the beef has cooked.

Remove the cooked beef to a board for carving and leave it to rest for at least 30 minutes before serving (while it's resting you can increase the heat in the oven to finish the roast potatoes if you're serving them). This resting period allows most of the juices which have bubbled up to the surface of the meat to seep back into it, and the meat itself firms up to make it easier to carve. Some of the juices will escape, though, and these should be poured into the gravy.

Traditional roast sirloin of beef

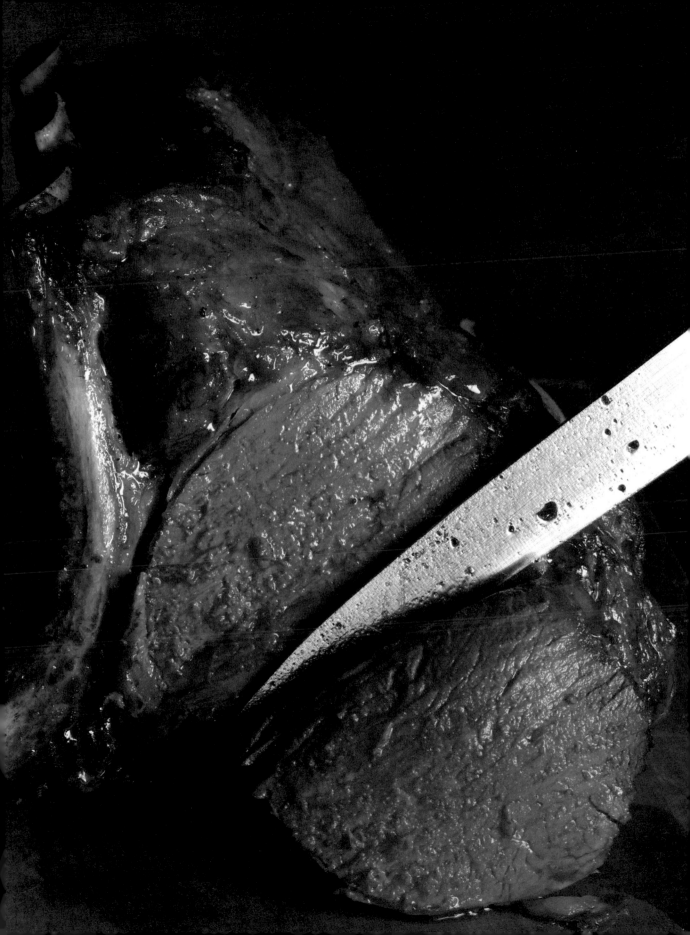

GRAVY *for* ROAST BEEF

·

SERVES 8 PEOPLE

When cooking classic roast beef the finishing touch is gravy made from all the escaped juices from the meat. It isn't difficult as long as you follow the instructions below.

1 heaped tablespoon plain flour	5 fl oz (150 ml) red wine or Sercial Madeira
1½ pints (850 ml) vegetable stock from potatoes or other vegetables	Salt and freshly milled black pepper

After removing the meat from the roasting tin, tilt the tin to see how much fat remains – you need about 2 tablespoons for this amount of gravy. If any more than this remains, spoon it into a dish. Place the roasting tin over a medium heat and sprinkle the flour into the fatty juices. Then with a wire whisk, blend in the flour using a circular movement. When you have a smooth paste, slowly add the vegetable water, whisking all the time and scraping the base of the tin to incorporate all the residue from the roast. Once the gravy has started to bubble, add the red wine or Madeira. Let the gravy continue to bubble very gently, then taste to see if it needs a little more seasoning. You can now pour the gravy into a jug and keep it warm if serving the meat is imminent, or, if not, leave it in the roasting tin and gently re-heat just before serving.

YORKSHIRE PUDDING

·

SERVES 4 PEOPLE

A classic Yorkshire pudding is not difficult to make provided you have the right recipe, the right size tin and the right oven temperature. I find a good solid roasting tin 11 × 7 inches (28 × 18 cm) makes a perfect pud for four people. So for eight, I double the ingredients and use two tins.

3 oz (75 g) plain flour	2 fl oz (50 ml) water
1 egg	Salt and freshly milled black pepper
3 fl oz (75 ml) milk	2 tablespoons beef dripping

Make up the batter by sifting the flour into a bowl and making a well in the centre. Break the egg into it and beat, gradually incorporating the flour, and then beat in the milk, water and seasoning (an electric hand whisk will do this in seconds). There is no need to leave the batter to stand, so make it when you're ready to cook the pudding.

About 15 minutes before the beef is due to come out of the oven, increase the heat to gas mark 7, 425°F (220°C), add the dripping to the roasting tin and place that on a baking sheet on a free shelf. After 15 minutes remove the meat, then place the tin over direct heat while you pour the batter into the sizzling hot fat. Return the tin to the baking sheet on the highest shelf (or, if you have roast potatoes on that one, the second highest). The pudding will take 25–30 minutes to rise and become crisp and golden. Serve as soon as possible: if it has to wait around too long it loses its crunchiness.

◆–●–◆

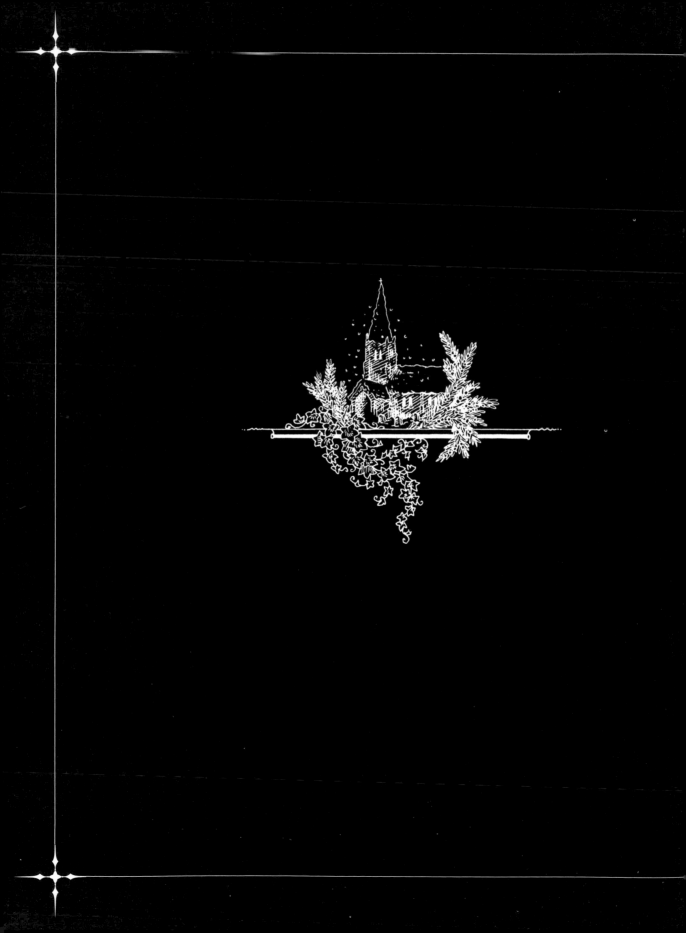

CHAPTER 8

Winter Vegetable Dishes AND Salads

Not everyone would agree with me perhaps, but it is my considered opinion that, with so many rich foods to be enjoyed at Christmas, it is best to keep the vegetables at least fairly simple. Another conclusion I have reached over the years is that in December our homegrown winter vegetables are at their very best, which makes me wonder why I ever bothered with the bland seasonless varieties that have become standard fare in supermarkets. The tight green Brussels sprouts, the earthy Fenland celery, the proud leeks, the squeaky red, white and green cabbages - all of them are far superior to the imported mange tout or courgettes or the fashionable anaemic 'baby' vegetables that have practically no flavour and cost a fortune.

For the same reason I have virtually abandoned buying salad ingredients at this time of year. Watercress or the small cherry tomatoes are fine for garnishes or canapés (see page 71), but lettuces, large tomatoes, cucumbers and even those designer salad leaves seem to be essentially gutless. As an alternative to salad I prefer to serve just some crisp celery and tart apples along with cheese and cold cuts, and rely on pickles and chutney to provide the meal with enough sharp contrast.

Party-givers therefore will only find a couple of seasonal salads in these pages, a cabbage coleslaw and a broccoli salad (see pages 149 and 148) – but I would also commend the Roasted red peppers stuffed with fennel (see page 98) which, served in a large shallow dish, will brighten and adorn any buffet party.

◆ ● ◆

CARAMELISED GLAZED ONIONS

·

SERVES 6 TO 8 PEOPLE

When the pressure is on, and there's a million and one things to do, peeling shallots is a fiddly affair requiring a great deal of patience. As little caramelised shallots have always been so very delicious, I initially compromised and cooked large Spanish onions, separated out into layers in the same way. Now it turns out there's no compromise because I actually prefer these to the shallots.

2 lb (1 kg) large Spanish onions	15 fl oz (425 ml) water
1½ oz (40 g) butter	¾ teaspoon salt
1½ oz (40 g) granulated sugar	

First of all peel the onions, then slice off the base root and cut them in quarters. Next separate the quarters into layers and place them in a large roomy saucepan along with the butter, sugar, water and salt. Bring them up to a steady simmer, then put a lid on and let them cook gently for about 15 minutes or until they take on a semi-transparent appearance. As soon as that happens take off the lid, turn the heat up to maximum and continue to cook, shaking the pan from time to time so that every piece of onion gets tossed in buttery liquid. Go on doing this until all the liquid has evaporated and the onions start to caramelise: at this stage keep tossing until eventually they turn a rich golden-brown and that's when they're ready to serve.

BRAISED CELERY VINAIGRETTE

·

SERVES 6 PEOPLE

*C*elery is a wonderful vegetable for serving with poultry or game birds. This particular recipe can be served hot with a main course or cold (that is, at room temperature) with cold cuts and salads. The English fenland celery – sometimes called dirty celery – has the finest flavour of all, and it is well worth the time spent scrubbing off the black earth.

3 heads celery	FOR THE VINAIGRETTE:
15 fl oz (425 ml) vegetable stock	3 tablespoons olive oil
5 fl oz (150 ml) dry white wine	1 tablespoon lemon juice
1 clove garlic, slightly crushed	2 rounded tablespoons fresh chopped
A strip lemon zest	parsley
¼ teaspoon celery seeds	½ teaspoon mixed pepper berries,
Salt and freshly milled black pepper	crushed (see page 56)

Begin by trimming the heads of celery back to 6 or 7 inches (15–18 cm) in length. Shave off the base of each head, and it may be necessary to strip off two or even three of the outer stalks if they're coarse or damaged (don't worry – all respectable trimmings can be used for stock or soup).

Now cut the heads into quarters lengthways and rinse them well in cold water, then drain them and arrange in a flameproof casserole (preferably one that can take the celery arranged flat in one layer). Now add the stock, wine, garlic, lemon zest and celery seeds plus a little freshly milled black pepper. Bring all this up to simmering point, then insert a double layer of greaseproof paper into the casserole so that it sits directly on top of the celery and comes 1 inch (2.5 cm) or so up the sides. Cover with a well-fitting lid and continue to simmer gently until the celery is tender – this will take about 1 hour, but do be sure it *is* tender because celery can be very deceptive and it is the one vegetable that should not be served *al dente!*

When it is tender use a draining spoon to remove the celery and arrange it in a shallow serving dish. Then briskly boil the juice remaining in the casserole (without a lid) until reduced to only some 2 or 3 tablespoons. Now remove the casserole from the heat and stir in all the vinaigrette ingredients. Taste and season with salt, then pour the sauce over the celery. Serve warm there and then or else cooled to room temperature.

◆◆◆

A butcher's bicycle piled high with poinsettias and red-berried holly, Oxford covered market.

BRUSSELS SPROUTS *in* RIESLING *with* BACON

·

SERVES 8 PEOPLE

*I*n Alsace cabbage is often braised in Riesling, a wine which also has an affinity with Brussels sprouts. If you can get tiny button sprouts for this so much the better, but in any event they should be tight and firm and not too large.

1½ lb (700 g) Brussels sprouts, prepared	2 shallots, finely chopped
4 oz (110 g) smoked bacon rashers with rinds	1 clove garlic, crushed
	6 fl oz (175 ml) Riesling
1 dessertspoon butter	Salt and freshly milled black pepper

Cut the rinds off the bacon rashers and, in your very largest frying-pan, melt the butter over a gentle heat. Keeping the heat to a minimum, add the bacon rinds to the pan and let them gently cook and release their fat which will permeate the butter. Meanwhile snip the bacon rashers into small pieces, then add them to the pan along with the shallots and garlic to begin cooking.

While that's happening, place the sprouts in a steamer, sprinkle them with salt, and steam them over boiling water for 4 minutes or so which should be enough just to half-cook them. After that turn the heat up under the frying-pan, add the sprouts and toss them around for 2 or 3 minutes or until they begin to take on a little colour. Now turn the heat up high, pour in the wine and let it bubble and reduce while you constantly turn the sprouts over and over to soak up the flavour of the wine. As soon as the sprouts are tender and the wine has reduced to about 2 tablespoons, transfer them to a serving dish, add a little freshly milled pepper and serve straightaway.

◆–◆–◆

PURÉE *of* POTATO *and* CELERIAC *with* GARLIC

·

SERVES 8 PEOPLE

This is a beautiful combination of flavours and perfect, as all purées are, for serving with braised dishes that have lots of sauce. Because you don't want to be mashing potatoes at the point when your guests are just arriving, we tested this, making it a couple of hours in advance and keeping it warm. There were no ill-effects whatsoever.

2 lb (1 kg) celeriac	5 fl oz (150 ml) double cream or crème fraîche
1 lb (450 g) potatoes	
2 fat cloves garlic, peeled	Salt and freshly milled black pepper
2 oz (50 g) butter	

First tackle the celeriac. You will need to have a bowl of cold water ready in which to put the prepared pieces to prevent it browning. Peel the celeriac thickly with a knife. Then cut into approximately ¾ inch (2 cm) cubes. Leave these pieces in the water whilst preparing the potatoes. Peel and cut these into 1 inch (2.5 cm) cubes – i.e. slightly larger than the celeriac. Now place the prepared vegetables in separate saucepans with 1 clove garlic to each saucepan. Pour enough boiling water over the vegetables just to cover them, add salt and simmer them for about 10 minutes or until they are tender. Drain each vegetable in a colander, place them together in a large heat-proof mixing bowl and add the butter and cream or crème fraîche and some freshly milled black pepper. Next, using an electric hand whisk, whisk them to a purée using the slow speed to break them up, then the fast one to whisk them till smooth. Now taste and season the purée, then place the bowl in a roasting tin half-filled with barely simmering water and it will keep warm quite happily until your guests arrive.

NOTE: For a party these quantities can be doubled to serve 12 and kept warm in exactly the same way.

◆◆◆

PARMESAN-BAKED PARSNIPS

·

SERVES 8 PEOPLE

This is one of the nicest ways to serve parsnips, baked crisp and golden-brown in the oven with a Parmesan coating. They can be prepared well in advance, up to 24 hours, or they can even be prepared and frozen and will then cook perfectly if allowed to defrost first. This recipe also works very well with sweet potatoes.

2½ lb (1.25 kg) parsnips	Salt and freshly milled black pepper
6 oz (175 g) plain flour	Groundnut oil
2 oz (50 g) freshly grated Parmesan cheese	A knob of butter

PRE-HEAT THE OVEN TO GAS MARK 6, 400°F (200°C)

Begin by combining the flour, Parmesan cheese, salt and pepper in a mixing bowl. Peel the parsnips using a potato parer. Then halve and quarter them lengthways and cut each length in half across, so that you end up with smallish chunks. Cut out some of the tough woody centres. Now pop the parsnips in a saucepan, pour in enough boiling water just to cover them and add salt. Put on a lid, bring them to the boil and boil for 3 minutes. Meanwhile have a large kitchen tray ready. Then, as soon as they are ready, drain them in a colander and whilst they are still steaming drop a few at a time (with the aid of some kitchen tongs) into the flour and Parmesan mixture, shaking the bowl and moving them around so that they get a good even coating. As they are coated transfer them to the tray. Make sure you do them all fairly swiftly as the flour mixture will only coat them whilst they are still steamy! When they're all coated they are ready to cook or store in the refrigerator or freeze. Any leftover flour and Parmesan can be kept (sifted) in the fridge or freezer for another time. What is important is to have plenty in order to coat the parsnips quickly.

To bake them, place a large solid roasting tin in the oven to pre-heat and in it put enough groundnut oil just to cover the base and a knob of butter for flavour. Then, when the oven is ready, remove the tin and place it over direct heat (turned fairly low) and, again using tongs, place the parsnips quickly side by side in the tin. Tilt it and baste all the parsnips with hot fat, place the tin in the oven and bake them for 20 minutes, then turn them over, drain off any surplus fat (a bulb baster is good for this) and continue to bake for a further 15–20 minutes or until they are crisp and golden.

NOTE: If your roast potatoes are on the top shelf, these can cook beneath.

Parmesan-baked parsnips (see above).

TRADITIONAL BRAISED RED CABBAGE *with* APPLES

·

SERVES 10 TO 12 PEOPLE

This is a recipe I have been cooking for years. It's great because it can be made the day before and gently re-heated with no last-minute bother. It is a perfect accompaniment to venison, goose or pork (and if you have any left over it does wonders for bangers and mash).

2 lb (1 kg) red cabbage	¼ level teaspoon ground cinnamon
1 lb (450 g) onions, chopped small	¼ level teaspoon ground cloves
1 lb (450 g) cooking apples, peeled, cored and chopped small	3 tablespoons brown sugar
1 clove garlic, chopped very small	3 tablespoons wine vinegar
¼ whole nutmeg, freshly grated	½ oz (15 g) butter
	Salt and freshly milled black pepper

PRE-HEAT THE OVEN TO GAS MARK 2, 300°F (150°C)

First discard the tough outer leaves of the cabbage, cut it into quarters and remove the hard stalk. Then shred the rest of the cabbage finely, using your sharpest knife (although you can shred it in a food processor, I prefer to do it by hand: it doesn't come out so uniform). Next, in a fairly large casserole, arrange a layer of shredded cabbage seasoned with salt and pepper, then a layer of chopped onions and apples with a sprinkling of garlic, spices and sugar. Continue with these alternate layers until everything is in.

Now pour in the wine vinegar, then lastly add dots of butter on the top. Put a tight lid on the casserole and let it cook very slowly in the oven for 2–2½ hours, stirring everything around once or twice during the cooking. Red cabbage, once cooked, will keep warm without coming to any harm, and it will also re-heat very successfully. And, yes, it does freeze well so, all in all, it's a real winner of a recipe.

◆━◆━◆

BASHED NEEPS *and* CARROTS

·

SERVES 8 PEOPLE

The 'neep' in question is what we in the South call swede. The combination of finely chopped swede and carrots with a little butter and coarsely ground pepper is colourful and very good.

12 oz (350 g) carrots, cut into 1½ inch (4 cm) chunks	12 oz (350 g) swede, cut into 1½ inch (4 cm) sized chunks
1 teaspoon butter	Salt and freshly milled black pepper

Place the carrots and swede in a saucepan with some salt and enough boiling water just to cover the vegetables. Bring it up to the boil and simmer gently for about 15 minutes or until the vegetables are tender but not mushy. Drain them in a colander, then either delegate someone (men are more patient with these things) to chop and chop with a sharp knife until the vegetables are minutely chopped – or else pop them in a food processor and use the pulse button with caution. Transfer the vegetables to a warmed serving dish, chop in the butter and some freshly milled pepper, then serve.

SALT-CRUSTED MINI BAKED POTATOES *with* COLD CHIVE HOLLANDAISE

·

SERVES 10 TO 12 PEOPLE

These are excellent to serve at a fork-supper party, as they are so much easier to deal with than the unwieldy large jacket potatoes. The topping can vary, and for those with rather less time to spare for preparation I would recommend a soft cheese mixed with garlic and herbs, or else something called herb and onion dip (which is available in tubs from better supermarkets).

20 small red potatoes (approximately jumbo egg size)	A double quantity Quick blender hollandaise (see page 207)
Olive oil	6 rounded tablespoon chives or 2 × ½ oz (15 g) packs fresh chives, snipped
1 heaped tablespoon Maldon salt	

PRE-HEAT THE OVEN TO GAS MARK 5, 375°F (190°C)

First of all make up the hollandaise as per the recipe on page 207, then pour it into a small bowl and stir in the snipped chives. Cover the bowl with cling film and leave in the refrigerator until the sauce is cold and set.

Next scrub the potatoes thoroughly and dry them with a tea-towel, then leave them aside for the skins to dry completely (if you get ready-scrubbed potatoes, just wipe them with damp kitchen paper). When the skins are nice and dry prick them with a fork, then moisten your hands with oil and rub the potatoes to oil them all over. Put about 1 tablespoon Maldon salt in a bowl and swirl each potato in the salt to coat it lightly.

Place the potatoes on a baking sheet and bake for 1 hour, or until crisp and tender. Then, when you're ready to serve, cut a cross in the top of each potato and gently squeeze up from the base to open out the cut slightly (use a tea-towel to protect your hands). Arrange the potatoes together on a large warmed serving dish and quickly top each one with a spoonful of the chive hollandaise (or any of the other toppings mentioned above).

NOTE: If you'd like a lighter sauce for the potatoes make 1 quantity of hollandaise and mix it with an equal quantity of fromage frais.

◆–◆–◆

Salt-crusted mini baked potatoes with cold chive hollandaise (see above).

BROCCOLI SALAD *with* SESAME DRESSING

·

SERVES 10 PEOPLE

*T*his crunchy salad keeps beautifully, so can easily be prepared in advance. It has a lovely colour that contrasts attractively with the Four star slaw (see page opposite) if you're serving both salads together.

2½ lb (1.25 kg) broccoli heads	2 tablespoons medium dry sherry
	1 teaspoon brown sugar
FOR THE DRESSING:	1 clove garlic, crushed
2 tablespoons light soy sauce	Salt and freshly milled black pepper
1 tablespoon sesame oil	1 tablespoon sesame seeds to garnish
3 tablespoons olive oil	

Combine all the ingredients for the dressing in a large bowl, then taste and season with salt only if it needs it: usually soy sauce provides quite enough saltiness.

Now prepare the broccoli by cutting the individual florets from the stalks – they need to be no bigger than a 5p piece to make them easier to serve. Place them in a colander and rinse well, then transfer them to a steamer and steam for 3–5 minutes or until they're tender but by no means soft. Transfer them immediately to the bowl containing the dressing and mix gently. After they have cooled, cover and chill until ready to serve. Just before serving sprinkle with the sesame seeds.

◆ ● ◆

FOUR STAR SLAW

·

SERVES 10 PEOPLE

The four 'stars' in this case are celeriac, carrot, cabbage and spring onion. The result is a very crunchy fresh-tasting salad that can be made the day before, if you cover it with cling film and keep it in the refrigerator until needed.

FOR THE DRESSING:	
5 fl oz (150 ml) soured cream	8 oz (225 g) celeriac, peeled and coarsely grated
2 cloves garlic, crushed	8 oz (225 g) carrots, peeled and grated
2 tablespoons mayonnaise	8 oz (225 g) white cabbage, finely shredded
2 tablespoons natural yoghurt	
1 teaspoon mustard powder	6 spring onions, finely chopped (including the green parts)
2 tablespoons olive oil	
1 tablespoon white wine vinegar	Poppy seeds to garnish
1 tablespoon lemon juice	
Salt and freshly milled black pepper	

Begin by combining the soured cream with the garlic, mayonnaise, yoghurt and mustard powder. Then mix together the oil, vinegar and lemon juice, and gradually whisk these into the soured cream mixture. Finally taste and season with salt and pepper.

Next, to prepare the salad, simply combine all the grated, shredded and chopped vegetables in a bowl, then pour over the dressing and toss with forks to mix thoroughly. Taste at this stage, as it may need more seasoning, then cover and chill. Toss again and sprinkle with poppy seeds just before serving.

◆▬◆▬◆

CHAPTER 9

Christmas Desserts
AND
Sweet Dishes

Whatever January may hold in the way of austerity or rigorous regimes, December is most definitely not the month for dieting. If, like me, you are constantly torn for the rest of the year between a passion for good food and an urgency to try and stay reasonably slim, you really have to regard Christmas as a holiday and a respite from the struggle!

At other times I am determined to pass on dessert courses at restaurants. Sometimes I weaken, only to be so often disappointed and then curse myself for having consumed so many calories on something that was not nearly so good as it sounded on the menu. This recurring experience has made me resolved to ensure that all the Christmas dessert recipes here are worth their weight (if you'll excuse the expression). So whatever the scales tell you in January, it will have been worth it.

Homemade ice creams and sorbets: Because I have an aversion to having too many gadgets in the kitchen I long resisted buying an ice-cream maker. But now, I confess, I am the owner of a very simple yet effective ice-cream maker, which dispenses with the bother of removing the ice cream from the freezer at the critical stage, of chilling bowls and re-whipping and so on. I would go so far as to say, in fact, that an ice-cream maker (cost approximately £50) would be an excellent Christmas present, either to give or receive!

In the absence of a machine, ice cream should be frozen in chilled shallow polythene boxes with the freezer switched to its coldest setting. A couple of hours later, when the ice cream is just beginning to set, empty it into a chilled bowl and whisk (preferably with an electric hand whisk), then return it to the freezer in its polythene container to finish freezing.

COFFEE GRANITA

·

SERVES 4 PEOPLE

This recipe has been given me by one of my favourite chefs, Simon Hopkinson from Bibendum restaurant in London. It's so simple, refreshing and very attractive served in stemmed glasses with lots of whipped cream.

1 pint (570 ml) strong espresso coffee (made in an espresso coffee-maker) or extremely strong filter coffee (the dark Continental roast is best)	4 oz (110 g) granulated sugar
	You will need a shallow 1½ pint (850 ml) polythene freezer container.

Begin by dissolving the sugar in the hot coffee. Allow it to cool, then pour it into a container and place it in the freezer. As soon as it has begun to form ice crystals around the edge, stir it with a fork to distribute the ice. (In a conventional freezer it can take 2–3 hours to reach this stage – so keep an eye on it.) After that keep returning and forking the ice crystals around until you have no liquid coffee left. This can take up to another 3 hours, but it is impossible to be exact as freezers vary.

You can serve the Coffee granita at this point, or, if you need to leave it frozen, all you do is remove it to the main body of the fridge 20 minutes before serving. To break up the ice, use a strong fork: this is not meant to be like a sorbet, but is served as coffee-flavoured ice crystals. Topped with whipped cream, it is a lovely refreshing way to end a good meal.

◆■◆

TRUFFLE TORTE

·

SERVES 10 PEOPLE

*T*his recipe is quite simply the best chocolate dessert I have tasted in years (see opposite) – and quite the easiest to make. The recipe was generously given to me by Derek Fuller, chef at the Athenaeum Hotel in Piccadilly, and has proved a winner with everyone who has tried it. It is very rich, though, so serve small portions!

5 tablespoons liquid glucose (available from chemists)	TO SERVE:
	Cocoa powder for dusting
5 tablespoons rum	Chilled single pouring cream
1 lb (450 g) plain dessert chocolate or luxury cooking chocolate – the best quality possible	You will need a 9 inch (23 cm) cake tin, lined with a circle of greaseproof or silicone paper, and the base and sides
1 pint (570 ml) double cream, at room temperature	lightly brushed with groundnut oil.
3 oz (75 g) Amaretti biscuits, crushed finely with a rolling pin	

Start off by sprinkling the crushed biscuits all over the base of the tin. Next break the chocolate into sections and put them in a heat-proof bowl together with the liquid glucose and the rum. Fit the bowl over a pan of barely simmering water, then leave it until the chocolate has melted and become quite smooth. Stir, then take off the heat and leave the mixture to cool for 5 minutes or so until it feels just warm.

Now, in a separate bowl, beat the cream until only very slightly thickened. Fold half into the chocolate mixture and then fold that mixture into the rest of the cream. When it is smoothly blended, spoon it into the prepared tin. Tap the tin gently to even the mixture out, cover with cling film and chill overnight.

Just before serving run a palette knife round the edge to loosen the torte, then give it a good shake and turn the whole thing out on to a serving plate (don't be nervous about this – it's very well behaved). To serve, dust the surface with sifted cocoa powder and, if you like, mark the top into serving sections. Have some chilled pouring cream to go with it; if you have any, a couple of tablespoons of Amaretti liqueur make a wonderful addition to the cream.

NOTE: The torte does freeze well, but since you can also make it a couple of days in advance, this doesn't really seem necessary.

Truffle torte (see above).

LITTLE STICKY TOFFEE PUDDINGS *with* PECAN TOFFEE SAUCE

·

SERVES 8 PEOPLE

This is as wicked as it sounds. A truly delectable combination of flavours and textures which are light and melt in the mouth (see page 158)! I would choose this as a Christmas or New Year dinner-party dessert, as the puddings freeze well and are no trouble to re-heat.

FOR THE PUDDINGS:	4 oz (110 g) butter
3 oz (75 g) butter, at room temperature	6 tablespoons double cream
5 oz (150 g) caster sugar	1 oz (25 g) pecan nuts, chopped
2 eggs, size 2, beaten	
6 oz (175 g) self-raising flour, sifted	TO SERVE:
6 oz (175 g) stoned dates, chopped	Chilled pouring cream
6 fl oz (175 ml) boiling water	
½ teaspoon vanilla essence	You will need eight 6 oz (175 g) metal
2 teaspoons coffee essence	pudding basins (see page 219) or eight
¾ teaspoon bicarbonate of soda	3 inch (7.5 cm) ramekin dishes, lightly
	oiled with groundnut oil, a Swiss-roll tin,
FOR THE SAUCE:	and a baking sheet.
6 oz (175 g) soft brown sugar	

PRE-HEAT THE OVEN TO GAS MARK 4, 350°F (180°C)

Begin by putting the chopped dates in a bowl and pouring boiling water over them. Then add the vanilla, coffee essence and bicarbonate of soda, and leave on one side. Next in a large mixing bowl, cream the butter and sugar together, beating (preferably with an electric hand whisk) until the mixture is pale, light and fluffy. Now gradually add the beaten eggs, a little at a time, beating well after each addition. After that carefully and lightly fold in the sifted flour using a metal spoon, and then you can fold in the date mixture (including the liquid). You'll probably think at this stage that you've done something wrong, because the mixture will look very sloppy, but don't worry: that is perfectly correct and the slackness of the mixture is what makes the pudding so light. Now divide the mixture equally between the eight containers, place them on a baking tray and bake in the centre of the oven for 25 minutes.

When they're cooked, leave them to cool for 5 minutes then, using a cloth to protect your hands, slide a small palette knife around each pudding and turn it out. If they have risen too much you may have to slice a little off the tops so that they can sit evenly on the plate (see the photograph on page 158). Now place the puddings on a shallow, Swiss roll-type, tin. Next make the sauce by combining all the ingredients in a saucepan and heating very gently until the sugar has melted and all the crystals have dissolved.

To serve the puddings: pre-heat the grill to its highest setting, and pour the sauce evenly over the puddings. Place the tin under the grill so the tops of the puddings are about 5 inches (13 cm) from the heat (knock off any nuts on the top to prevent them browning) and let them heat through for about 8 minutes. What will happen is the tops will become brown and slightly crunchy and the sauce will be hot and bubbling. Serve with chilled pouring cream – and sit back to watch the looks of ecstasy on the faces of your guests.

NOTE: After freezing, de-frost, pour the hot sauce over and re-heat.

OLD ENGLISH PORT WINE JELLY

·

SERVES 8 PEOPLE

After a rich main course nothing could be nicer and more refreshing to finish off the meal than this cool, light and fragrant jelly.

5 oz (150 g) granulated sugar	3 0.4 oz (11 g) packets powdered gelatine
1 pint (570 ml) water	15 fl oz (425 ml) good quality ruby port
1 stick cinnamon	5 fl oz (150 ml) light red wine
4 cloves	Frosted black grapes (see page 165)
1 blade mace	
The thinly pared zest and juice of 1 large lemon	You will need a 2¼ pint (1.35 litre) jelly mould or 8 stemmed glasses.

First place 5 oz (150 g) sugar in a saucepan along with 1 pint (570 ml) water and the cinnamon stick, cloves, mace and lemon zest and juice. Cover the pan and bring to the boil, then remove from the heat. Sprinkle in the gelatine, whisk and allow it to dissolve for 15 minutes, whisking again from time to time.

Now strain the spices and zest from the syrup. Then stir the port and wine into it, and at this stage taste it: the flavour should be strong and rather more sweet than you would normally have it – this sweetness lessens once the mixture is chilled. Stir in more sugar if you are sure it needs it and stir until dissolved. Now pour the liquid into the jelly mould or 8 stemmed glasses and leave to set. Serve slightly chilled and topped with frosted black grapes.

IRISH COFFEE PUDDING

·

SERVES 4 TO 6 PEOPLE

If you're having a dinner party and want to serve a lighter alternative to something rich, then this is a good bet. You can, of course, use Scotch whisky or brandy instead of Irish whiskey. What you finish up with is in fact an old-fashioned honeycomb mould which separates into layers as it sets.

1½ oz (40 g) fine-ground Italian espresso coffee	2 oz (50 g) sugar
	6 tablespoons single cream
3 tablespoons Irish whiskey	
3 eggs, size 1	TO SERVE:
15 fl oz (425 ml) milk	Chilled pouring cream
8 fl oz (225 ml) boiling water	Coffee and hazelnut macaroons
1 × 0.4 oz (11 g) sachet plus 1 teaspoon powdered gelatine	(see page 177)

You will need a 2½ pint (1.5 litre) mould.

First measure out 8 fl oz (225 ml) boiling water into a small saucepan, then stir in the coffee and place the pan on a gentle heat until the infusion starts to bubble around the edge of the pan. Remove from the heat and leave the coffee to infuse for 15 minutes. After that pour it into a fine coffee filter set over a coffee-pot and leave it to drip through.

While that's happening heat the milk to just below boiling point and remove from the heat. Next separate the eggs, putting the yolks into a heat-proof bowl and the whites into a large mixing bowl. Add the gelatine, sugar and cream to the egg yolks and whisk together very thoroughly. Now pour in the hot milk, whisking the mixture as you pour. Position the bowl over a saucepan of barely simmering water and cook the custard, stirring often, for 25–30 minutes until it is thick enough to coat the back of a spoon. Remove the bowl from over the water, stir in the whiskey and strained coffee, and leave until it is barely warm.

Whisk the egg whites till stiff, then stir them into the coffee-flavoured custard. Now pour everything into a 2½ pint (1.5 litre) mould, cover and chill for about 8 hours in the refrigerator.

To serve, loosen the soft top layer from the side of the mould, then invert on to a serving dish. Serve with chilled pouring cream and some Coffee and hazelnut macaroons (see page 177).

One little sticky toffee pudding with pecan toffee sauce (see page 156).

CHAMPAGNE JELLIES *with* SYLLABUB CREAM

·

MAKES 12

If you really want to splash out you can make this with champagne, but sparkling white wine works very well too. This is a lovely light dessert that slips down easily after a rich main course. It looks beautiful served in stemmed champagne flutes (see page 162): the quantities below will fill twelve stemmed glasses of 5 fl oz (150 ml) capacity, so if you only want six you can easily halve the recipe (but then you'll have to drink the rest of the champagne)!

FOR THE JELLY:	FOR THE SYLLABUB:
2 large lemons	2 tablespoons of the same wine (as above)
6 oz (175 g) caster sugar	1 tablespoon brandy
4 0.4 oz (11 g) packets powdered gelatine	The juice of ½ lemon
1 pint (570 ml) champagne or medium-dry sparkling white wine	1 oz (25 g) caster sugar
	5 fl oz (150 ml) double cream
1½ pints (900 ml) water	

TO DECORATE:
Frosted grapes (see page 165)

To make the jelly, pour 1½ pints (900 ml) water into a saucepan. Next scrub the lemons well, then pare off the coloured part only of the zest, using a peeler, add this to the pan together with the sugar and bring up to simmering point. After that take the pan off the heat and sprinkle in the gelatine, whisking the mixture with a balloon whisk at the same time.

Now leave this on one side to melt the gelatine, stirring once or twice to ensure that it has all dissolved into the liquid. Next add the juice of the lemons, then strain the contents of the pan either through a coffee filter or a fine sieve lined with muslin or gauze. Leave to cool, cover and chill in the refrigerator until the jelly is just on the point of setting – this should take about 1–1½ hours.

After that uncork the wine, measure out 1 pint (570 ml) and pour it into the jelly. Stir once or twice to blend everything, then ladle the jelly gently into the serving glasses (being gentle means trying to conserve as many bubbles as you can so that they will be apparent when the jelly is eaten). Chill the jellies, covered with cling film, for 4 hours – by which time they should have a deliciously soft set, not rubbery but firm enough to support the syllabub.

While the jelly is setting make the syllabub topping by combining 2 tablespoons wine, the brandy, lemon juice and sugar together in a bowl. Leave this on one side, stirring occasionally, until the sugar has dissolved. Then pour in the cream and whisk until it stands in soft peaks; cover and chill until you are ready to serve. Just before serving, top each jelly with blobs of the softly whipped cream and decorate with frosted grapes.

◆—◆—◆

WALNUT SHORTBREADS
(for ice cream)

·

MAKES APPROXIMATELY 20

These light, crumbly little biscuits are just the thing to serve with homemade ice creams. They could also be packed into boxes or jars for a homemade Christmas gift. Walnut shortbread can also be made in advance and then frozen.

4 oz (110 g) salted butter, at room temperature	2 oz (50 g) walnut pieces
	A little icing sugar for dusting
2 oz (50 g) caster sugar	
6 oz (175 g) plain flour, sifted	You will need a baking sheet, lightly
2 oz (50 g) rice flour	greased, and a 1¾ inch (4.5 cm) cutter.

PRE-HEAT THE OVEN TO GAS MARK 2, 300°F (150°C)

The first thing you need to do is grind the walnuts, which you can do very carefully using the 'pulse' switch on a food processor (if this is overdone the nuts go pasty and oily). Otherwise a hand-held nut grinder will do the job.

To make the shortbread, place the butter and sugar in a large mixing bowl and cream them together until pale and fluffy. Then mix the sifted flour and rice flour together and gradually work this into the creamed mixture, a tablespoonful at a time. Next add the ground walnuts and use your hands to form the mixture into a smooth dough. Leave the dough to rest in a plastic bag in the refrigerator for 30 minutes, then roll it out on a lightly floured working surface to a round approximately 8 inches (20 cm) in diameter.

Now, using a 1¾ inch (4.5 cm) cutter, cut out approximately 20 rounds, re-rolling the trimmings. Place them on a lightly greased baking sheet and bake in the oven for 45 minutes. Cool them for 5 minutes before transferring to a wire rack. When completely cool dust them with icing sugar and store in an airtight container.

MULLED WINE SORBET

·

MAKES 1¾ PINTS (1 LITRE)

T his is a truly special sorbet, perfect for serving to anyone suffering from a surfeit of Christmas indulgence. I am indebted to Caroline Liddell and Robin Weir for the recipe from their splendid book on ice creams.

6 oz (175 g) granulated sugar	1½ lemons
6 fl oz (175 ml) water	2 tablespoons ruby port
10 fl oz (275 ml) red wine	1 egg white, size 1
3 cloves	
¼ teaspoon ground cinnamon	You will need a 2½ pint (1½ litre) plastic freezer box.
⅛ teaspoon freshly grated nutmeg	
1 orange	

Begin by making a syrup. This you do by adding the sugar to the water, heating it in a saucepan to boiling point, stirring gently, then simmering for 15 minutes. Remove from the heat and allow to cool before pouring it into a bowl and chilling in the refrigerator.

Now, using a potato peeler, remove three strips of zest (coloured part only) from the orange and one of the lemons, then cut these finely across to give hair-like shreds. Squeeze the juice from all the citrus fruit. Next heat the wine, spices, orange and lemon juices together with the zest in a saucepan (not aluminium), simmer gently for 5 minutes, then leave to cool. When cool add the port, pour this into a separate bowl and put it into the refrigerator to chill (I often do this overnight).

When both liquids are completely chilled, add 8 fl oz (225 ml) of the syrup to the wine mixture, put it in an ice-cream maker and churn for 8 minutes. Meanwhile beat the egg white until foamy but not holding stiff peaks, then add that and continue to churn for about another 8 minutes (or according to the maker's instructions). Then place the sorbet in a plastic freezer box in the freezer till needed. If you don't have an ice-cream machine put the wine and syrup mixture into a rectangular plastic box and freeze, covered, for up to 2–3 hours or until it reaches the stage of becoming thicker, icy and opaque. Add the beaten egg whites at this stage (as above) and continue to freeze for a further 6–7 hours, stirring it at hourly intervals. The beauty of this sorbet is that you can serve it straight from the freezer as the alcohol gives it a nice soft consistency. Use within 1 month.

Champagne jellies with syllabub cream (see page 160) decorated with Frosted grapes (see page 165).

ICED CHOCOLATE CHESTNUT CREAMS *with* WHITE CHOCOLATE SAUCE

•

SERVES 8 PEOPLE

*T*his *is one of the best frozen dessert dishes ever. Not only do the creams look and taste very good but they are also easy to make and keep well for a good 5–6 weeks in the freezer, so that's one party dessert dish which can be taken care of well in advance. I think they look prettiest in little metal pudding basins (see page 219) but we've tried them in 3 inch (7.5 cm) ramekins and they go very well too.*

FOR THE CHOCOLATE LAYER:
3 oz (75 g) luxury dark dessert chocolate

1 tablespoon rum

2 egg yolks, size 1

1 egg white, size 1

FOR THE CENTRE:
5 fl oz (150 ml) double cream

1 × 8¾ oz (240 g) tin crème de marron
(sweetened chestnut purée)

1 egg white, size 1

FOR THE CHESTNUT LAYER:
1 × 8¾ oz (240 g) tin crème de marron

FOR THE WHITE CHOCOLATE SAUCE:
10 fl oz (275 ml) single cream

2 oz (50 g) good quality white chocolate,
chopped

FOR THE DECORATION:
8 pieces candied chestnut (marron glacé)

You will need eight metal pudding basins of 5 fl oz (150 ml) capacity or eight 3 inch (7.5 cm) ramekins, lightly oiled.

Begin with the chocolate layer by breaking up the chocolate and placing it in a small basin along with the rum. Then fit the basin over a pan containing about 1 inch (2.5 cm) of barely simmering water; it's important that the basin doesn't come in contact with the water. As soon as the chocolate has melted, remove it from the heat and beat in the egg yolks. Then, using a clean whisk, beat the egg white to the soft peak stage and fold it carefully into the chocolate. Now spoon an equal quantity of the chocolate mixture into each little container. This, when it's turned out, will be the top layer. Now place the containers in the freezer (I always put them in a Swiss-roll tin for easy management) and leave them to freeze for about 1 hour.

Meanwhile make the second layer by emptying the contents of the first tin of chestnut purée into a small basin. Beat it with a fork to even it and soften it

164

up a bit, then in another bowl whisk the double cream until it's
but floppy; it's very important not to overdo it. Now fold the crea
chestnut purée thoroughly and evenly until all the marbling has dis
Next wash the whisk in warm soapy water to remove all traces of gr
thoroughly, and in a clean bowl whisk the egg white until it reach
peak stage. Now fold it gently and carefully into the chestnut mixt
will then be ready to spoon over the frozen chocolate mixture in the small containers. Freeze them again for 1 hour.

Finally whip the contents of the second tin of chestnut purée and spoon this
over to make the final layer. Cover the little pots with cling film and freeze until
you need them. You can either leave the desserts in the pots, or as soon as
they're frozen turn them out by sliding a knife all round the inside of each container and re-packing them in cling film to store without their containers in a
freezer box.

To make the white chocolate sauce, gently warm half the cream in a small
saucepan. When it's just hot enough for you to hold your little finger in it,
remove it from the heat, add the chopped chocolate and stir until it's melted.
Then add the remaining cream, cool, cover and store in the refrigerator till
needed.

To serve the chestnut creams remove them from the freezer to the main
body of the refrigerator 15 minutes before they're needed. Then serve in a pool
of white chocolate sauce and decorate each with a piece of marron glacé.

◆ ● ◆

FROSTED GRAPES

4–5 oz (110–150 g) seedless grapes	Caster sugar
1 egg white	Silicone paper

What you need to do for the prettiest effect is to try to separate the grapes into
bunches of two or three (depending on their size), leaving them still attached
to the stalk (see the photograph on page 162). Then wash and dry them
thoroughly and dip them first into egg white and then into the sugar, making
sure each one gets an even coating of sugar. Spread them on silicone paper to
dry for a couple of hours before using to decorate. They look superb on Champagne jellies with syllabub cream (see page 160).

◆ ● ◆

BÛCHE *de* NOËL
Chocolate Chestnut Log

·

SERVES 8 TO 10 PEOPLE

This famous French confection turns up in a number of guises, some of which I have a great aversion to, having never liked the sickly sweet butter cream that's often used for the icing. However, I do have a great passion for more sophisticated chocolaty chestnut desserts, so here I'm offering a lighter version which makes an excellent party dessert.

FOR THE BASE:

6 eggs, size 1

5 oz (150 g) caster sugar

2 oz (50 g) cocoa powder, sifted

A little icing sugar

FOR THE FILLING:

1 × 8¾ oz (240 g) tin crème de marron (sweetened chestnut purée)

4 whole candied chestnuts (marron glacé), roughly chopped

1 tablespoon double cream

FOR THE DECORATION:

10 fl oz (275 ml) double cream, less 1 tablespoon (see above)

2 oz (50 g) dark dessert chocolate

A few holly leaves

You will need a Swiss-roll tin 13 × 9 inches (32 × 23 cm), greased and lined with silicone paper.

PRE-HEAT THE OVEN TO GAS MARK 4, 350°F (180°C)

First make the base by separating the eggs – put the whites in a large bowl and the yolks in a smaller bowl. Then, using an electric hand whisk, whisk the egg yolks until they start to pale and thicken, add the sugar and continue to whisk until the mixture becomes more thickened (do not overdo this or it will go too stiff). Now whisk in the cocoa powder until it's thoroughly blended in.

Next wash the whisk heads in warm soapy water and, when they are absolutely dry, clean and grease-free, whisk the egg whites until they form soft peaks. Spoon one lot of egg white into the chocolate mixture to loosen it, then begin carefully to fold all the chocolate mixture into the egg whites, cutting and folding until they're thoroughly combined. Spread the mixture into the prepared tin, giving it a few taps to even it out, and bake it in the centre of the oven for about 20 minutes or until it is risen and puffy and feels springy in the centre – it's important not to overcook. When you take it out of the oven it will sink down quite a lot but that's quite in order, so don't panic.

Let it cool completely, then place a sheet of greaseproof or silicone paper, about 1 inch (2.5 cm) larger all round than the Swiss-roll tin, on a work surface

166

and sprinkle it with some icing sugar. Loosen the edges of the chocolate base all round, turn it out on to the paper and carefully peel off the base paper.

Now for the filling: simply empty the contents of the chestnut purée into a bowl, add 1 tablespoon double cream and mix thoroughly. Then, using a small palette knife, spread the mixture carefully and evenly all over the base. After that sprinkle the chopped candied chestnuts all over.

The next thing you need to do is have ready a plate that the whole length of the log will sit comfortably on (an oval meat plate can be used or you could line a small oblong tray with foil). Now, taking the edge of the greaseproof or silicone paper to guide you, roll the base over *lengthways* into a long roll, keeping it on the edge of the paper; then, transferring it to the plate, pull away the last of the paper. If it cracks or loses its shape don't worry: just pat it back into a log shape using your hands (nothing will show because of the topping). If you want to freeze it at this stage, keep it in the paper then wrap it in foil.

Now to make an authentic-looking log you need to cut two diagonal pieces off each end; these are to represent branches and should be about 2 inches (5 cm) at their widest part. Place one on one side of the log, cut side to join it, and the other on the other side but this time nearer the top (see below). You'll find the sticky chestnut cream will make these two weld on to the rest OK. Now you have a log shape, all you require is some Christmas snow. For this you need to melt the chocolate in a bowl over some hot water, then beat the rest of the 10 fl oz (275 ml) cream till it's spreadable – be careful not to overbeat. Now spread the cream evenly all over the log. Then drizzle a little trickle of melted chocolate up and down the length of the cream, take a fork and, working only lengthways, blend the chocolate lightly into the cream, giving a woody bark-like effect. The 'branches' need the chocolate swirled round with the fork at the ends, as do the ends of the log. I also like to put fresh holly on the plate.

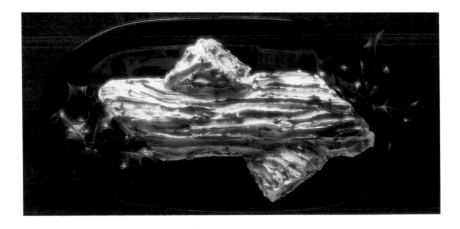

Bûche de Noël.

167

CARAMELISED ORANGE TRIFLE

·

SERVES 8 TO 10 PEOPLE

I have been making the same Christmas trifle for years on end – but this year I decided to experiment with something new, without totally sacrificing the traditional qualities we'd grown to love. This fits the bill perfectly (see page 171).

FOR THE TRIFLE BASE:	FOR THE CUSTARD:
5 trifle sponges	5 egg yolks, size 1
2–3 tablespoons Seville orange marmalade	1 teaspoon cornflour
5 fl oz (150 ml) Sercial Madeira	15 fl oz (425 ml) double cream
2 bananas	1 oz (25 g) caster sugar
	A few drops pure vanilla extract

FOR THE CARAMEL ORANGES:	FOR THE TOPPING:
3 large Navel oranges	10 fl oz (275 ml) double cream, whipped
The grated zest of 1 of the oranges	2 tablespoons hazelnuts, lightly toasted under the grill and roughly chopped
1 tablespoon Cognac	
1 tablespoon orange juice	
2 tablespoons soft dark brown sugar	You will need a 3 pint (1.75 litre) glass bowl.

First of all split the sponges in half lengthways, spread each half with marmalade, then re-form them into sandwiches. Spread the top of each sandwich with marmalade, cut each one across into three, then arrange the pieces in the base of the glass bowl. Now make a few stabs in the sponges with a sharp knife and carefully pour the Madeira all over them, distributing it as evenly as you can – then leave on one side for the sponges to soak it all up.

Next grate the zest from one of the oranges and keep on one side. Place each orange on a board and, using your sharpest knife, pare off all the skin and pith. Then, holding each orange in one hand over a bowl to catch the juices – you will need 1 tablespoon for the caramel – cut out the segments by slicing the knife in at the line of pith which divides the segments (you need to cut each segment out with the pithy membrane left behind). Cut each segment in half and place in a small bowl together with the grated zest.

To make the caramel, dissolve the 2 tablespoons soft brown sugar with 1 tablespoon of the reserved orange juice in a small pan over a gentle heat, and as soon as the crystals have dissolved turn the heat up to caramelise the mixture: it is ready when it turns one shade darker and looks syrupy and slightly thicker than before. Remove the pan from the heat and add the Cognac – this will make it splutter a bit, but that's OK. Pour the caramel mixture over the oranges.

Next make the custard. This you do by mixing the egg yolks, sugar, cornflour and vanilla extract in a basin, then in a saucepan bring the cream up to simmering point and pour it over the egg mixture. Whisk well, return the whole lot to the saucepan and re-heat gently, still whisking, until the custard has thickened (don't worry if it looks curdled at this stage: the addition of the cornflour will ensure that it will eventually become smooth once off the heat, if you work at it with the whisk).

Let the custard cool, and meanwhile strain the oranges, reserving the caramel juice. Arrange the oranges in amongst the sponge cakes in the trifle bowl, tipping it from side to side to make sure all the Madeira has soaked in. Now slice the bananas thinly and scatter these into the bowl, and push them down the sides as well. Next add the caramel juice to the custard and pour this on top of everything in the bowl. Cover with cling film and chill for several hours before topping the trifle with the whipped cream and scattering this with the toasted hazelnuts. Keep the trifle covered in the refrigerator and serve chilled.

CINNAMON ICE CREAM

·

MAKES 1¾ PINTS (1 LITRE)

You can happily serve this ice cream on its own, but you'll find it also has a marvellous affinity with lots of other Christmassy flavours. It makes a wonderful contrast, for instance, with Christmas dried fruit compote (see page 175) or Lattice mincemeat dessert tart (see page 53) – but perhaps its star performance is as an accompaniment to the Apple, mincemeat and nut strudel (see page 52).

6 egg yolks, size 1	1 level teaspoon ground cinnamon
4 oz (110 g) caster sugar	10 fl oz (275 ml) double cream
1 pint (570 ml) milk	2 slightly rounded teaspoons custard
1 stick cinnamon	powder

First of all place the egg yolks, sugar and custard powder in a bowl and whisk them with an electric hand whisk (or balloon whisk) until the mixture has become pale and thickened. Next put the milk, cinnamon stick and ground cinnamon in a saucepan, bring the mixture up just to simmering point, then pour it on to the egg mixture, whisking all the while as you pour.

Return the custard to the saucepan and continue whisking over a gentle heat until the custard has thickened. Don't worry about curdling – if it does separate, as soon as you pour it back into a bowl and continue to whisk it *will* become smooth again: the custard powder acts as an excellent stabiliser. Pour the custard into a bowl and, when cool, cover with a piece of cling film directly on the surface of the custard and extended up the side of the bowl (to prevent a skin forming). Chill thoroughly in the refrigerator or overnight.

Next day, whip the cream to the soft shape stage, then fold it into the custard (you can now discard the cinnamon stick). The ice cream can now be churned in an ice-cream maker for 20 minutes until it is soft and velvety. Alternatively pour it into a plastic freezer box (approximately 9 × 6 inches, 23 × 15 cm), cover the surface with cling film, put a lid on and freeze. Thereafter re-mix with a fork every 30 minutes until it reaches the right consistency. The ice cream should be eaten within 3 weeks; before serving, remove it to the main body of the refrigerator for 20 minutes to soften.

◆ ◆

Caramelised orange trifle (see page 168).

FIG ICE CREAM

·

MAKES 1½ PINTS (900 ML)

T̶ruly this is an inspired ice cream, one which I first encountered on a trip to Paris at Christmas, where I ate it with a Compote of prunes in port (see page opposite). The two together seem to encapsulate all the flavours of Christmas (see page 174).

12 oz (350 g) no-soak dried figs	4 oz (110 g) caster sugar
10 fl oz (275 ml) water	½ teaspoon pure vanilla extract
1 oz (25 g) soft brown sugar	1 rounded teaspoon custard powder
1 pint (570 ml) milk	2 tablespoons brandy
4 egg yolks, size 1	5 fl oz (150 ml) double cream

First place the figs and brown sugar in a medium-sized saucepan and add the water. Bring this up to simmering point and simmer gently with a lid on for about 5 minutes, then uncover and continue to simmer for a further 5 minutes or until the figs are plump and tender. Now remove from the heat, replace the lid and leave them until they're completely cold.

The next stage is to purée the figs, so drain off the cooking liquid, snip off and discard the tops of the figs, then place them either in a liquidiser or a food processor along with the milk and blend them until they have become smooth and uniform. Now press the mixture through a sieve to extract any tough resistant pieces of skin.

Next make the custard by whisking the egg yolks, custard powder, caster sugar and vanilla extract thoroughly together. Now bring the milk and fig mixture up to the boil, then pour it on to the egg yolk mixture. Return the whole lot to the saucepan and bring it back to the boil gently, still stirring with a whisk to keep it smooth. If it looks like curdling, don't worry: just whisk it together again as it cools (the custard powder is there to keep it stabilised).

Now let the custard cool before combining it with the brandy and the double cream (lightly whipped until it just holds its shape). Place the mixture in an ice-cream maker and churn according to the maker's instructions – you will probably have to do this in two batches. If you don't have an ice-cream maker then whip it by hand as soon as it freezes. Pack the ice cream into a storage container and store in the freezer until ready to use. Before serving remove it to the refrigerator for 30 minutes to soften.

Prune Ice Cream

This can be made in exactly the same way as the Fig ice cream opposite, using 12 oz (350 g) no-soak prunes instead of figs, and leaving out the vanilla. Cook no-soak prunes in 15 fl oz (425 ml) cold water for the slightly longer time of 20 minutes. If you have Armagnac, this would be a lovely addition in place of the brandy, and the ice cream would make a superb accompaniment to Compote of figs in port (see page 217).

COMPOTE *of* PRUNES *in* PORT

SERVES 6 PEOPLE (with Fig ice cream)

Because a recipe is simple, it's easy to pass it by (like not trying on something that doesn't look much on the hanger). However, this practical recipe tastes as good as if you had spent hours preparing it (see page 174). It can be served just with cream or Greek yoghurt, but I think it has a heavenly affinity with Fig ice cream.

1 lb (450 g) Californian no-soak stoned prunes	1 orange
1 pint (570 ml) water	2 oz (50 g) granulated sugar
	5 fl oz (150 ml) port

Use a potato peeler to pare off the coloured part only of the orange zest then, using a sharp knife, cut this into little shreds. After that squeeze out the orange juice, then place the prunes, orange juice and zest in a bowl. Add 1 pint (570 ml) water, stir everything around, and leave it on one side for 2 hours.

Next pour the contents of the bowl into a saucepan, add the sugar and simmer very gently for 1 hour (without a lid): it should only *just* simmer, so have a look from time to time to make sure the liquid does not all evaporate. At the end of the cooking time pour the whole lot into a serving bowl and, while it is still hot, stir in the port. Allow the prunes to cool completely in this liquid, and chill before serving.

CHRISTMAS DRIED FRUIT COMPOTE

·

SERVES 8 PEOPLE

This, if you like, is all the Christmas pudding flavours without the pudding. It is light, fragrant and very fruity. Serve it well chilled with some lightly whipped cream or – better still – with Cinnamon ice cream (see page 170).

4 oz (110 g) no-soak dried apricots	10 fl oz (275 ml) cold water
4 oz (110 g) no-soak dried figs, halved	12 fl oz (350 ml) tawny port
4 oz (110 g) no-soak prunes	
4 oz (110 g) raisins	TO SERVE:
2 oranges	2 oz (50 g) sliced almonds, lightly toasted

First of all rinse the apricots, figs and prunes under cold, running water, then place them in a large saucepan. Next scrub one of the oranges, slice it into very thin rounds, and cut each round into four. Add these, together with the raisins, to the rest of the fruit in the pan, pour in the cold water and simmer (covered) for 15 minutes. Meanwhile squeeze the juice from the other orange and, when the fruit is cooked, stir in the orange juice and the port. Leave the compote to cool and, before serving, chill in the refrigerator for 24 hours so all the flavours can develop. Serve sprinkled with the toasted nuts.

◆-◆-◆

Fig ice cream (see page 172) with Compote of prunes in port (see page 173).

INDIVIDUAL PECAN PIES

·

SERVES 8 PEOPLE

Once on a holiday in New England I found it very hard to order any dessert other than pecan pie. Since then I have loved to try out all the different variations of this classic – and this one here achieves, I feel, just the right degree of moist stickiness. Serve the pies warm either with chilled whipped cream (perhaps lightened with an equal quantity of Greek yoghurt) or with some well chilled fromage frais.

FOR THE PASTRY:	7 oz (200 g) golden syrup
6 oz (175 g) plain flour	1½ (40 g) butter, melted
1½ level tablespoons icing sugar	1 tablespoon rum
3 oz (75 g) salted butter, softened	6 oz (175 g) pecan nut halves, roughly
1 egg yolk, size 1	chopped
Approximately 3 tablespoons very cold water	24 pecan nut halves for decoration
	You will need eight 4 inch (10 cm) patty or
FOR THE FILLING:	Yorkshire pudding tins, ¾ inch (2 cm)
3 eggs, size 2	deep, lightly greased, and 2 solid baking
4 oz (110 g) soft dark brown sugar	sheets.

PRE-HEAT THE OVEN TO GAS MARK 5, 375°F (190°C)

Begin by making the pastry: sift the dry ingredients into a mixing bowl, then add the softened butter cut into nut-sized pieces, and rub them in until the mixture resembles fine breadcrumbs. Now in a small bowl combine the egg yolk with 3 tablespoons very cold water, then stir this into the mixture with a fork and when it begins to form clumps start pressing the dough together with your hands to form a ball. Put the dough into a plastic bag and transfer it to the refrigerator for 45 minutes – the chilling will make it much easier to handle.

Place two solid baking sheets in the oven to pre-heat. When the pastry has chilled roll it out on a lightly floured surface to a thickness of just under ⅛ inch (3 mm). Use a 5 inch (13 cm) diameter lid or saucer to help you, cut out 8 rounds, re-rolling the trimmings as necessary. Line the patty tins with the rounds, gently easing them into the tins to avoid stretching the pastry. Now distribute the chopped pecans evenly into the pastry cases.

Next break the eggs into a large mixing bowl and whisk until foamy, then stir in the brown sugar, syrup, melted butter and rum. Beat well to mix together, then spoon the mixture equally into the patty tins, bringing it up to approximately ⅛ inch (3 mm) from the top. Place three pecan halves on top of each pie

176

and transfer them to the oven to bake on the baking sheets for 25–30 minutes. When cooked the pies will have a very puffed-up, almost exploded appearance, but after 5 minutes' cooling, they will gradually subside. Remove them to a wire rack to finish cooling. I think they actually taste stickier if you eat them the next day – in which case re-heat slightly before serving.

—◆•◆—

COFFEE *and* HAZELNUT MACAROONS

•

MAKES APPROXIMATELY 30

These crunchy little hazelnut biscuits go very well with Irish coffee pudding (see page 159). Alternatively, if you leave out the coffee, they're excellent for serving with ice creams or jellies. You can also make very tiny biscuits and serve them in cases as petits fours to go with coffee. They also freeze well, so it's useful to have a little stock of them to serve with ice cream.

4 oz (110 g) hazelnuts, skinned	2 level tablespoons powdered instant coffee
8 oz (225 g) caster sugar	
2 heaped teaspoons ground rice	
2 egg whites, size 1	You will need 2 baking sheets and some edible rice paper.

PRE-HEAT THE OVEN TO GAS MARK 2, 300°F (150°C)

First the nuts need to be ground to a coarse meal consistency: this can be done in a food processor using the 'pulse' action – but do be careful because one pulse too many and they become very oily. Alternatively you can use a small-handled nut grinder.

Put the ground nuts in a mixing bowl together with the sugar and ground rice, and mix them well together. Then stir in the unbeaten egg whites and the coffee powder and continue to mix to a stiffish paste. Now line two baking sheets with the rice paper and put teaspoonfuls of the biscuit mixture on them, leaving room in between them for expansion during the cooking. Bake in the oven for 30–35 minutes or until they are crisp on top. Leave to cool completely before lifting the biscuits from the baking sheet, and store in an airtight tin until needed.

—◆•◆—

CHAPTER 10

Homemade Sweets

AND

Chocolates

Why bother to make your own, you ask, when the shops and super-markets are filled to overflowing with commercially produced chocolates? Well, it is my opinion that mass-production has succeeded in only one thing, and that is in reducing the quality of our chocolates. The majority of what is bought nowadays is sickly sweet, supplemented with saccharine, and minimal in its content of cocoa solids or cocoa butter.

There are honourable exceptions and, if you're lucky enough to live within range of a really good specialist chocolate shop, you might have no difficulty in finding something dark and delicious to serve with the coffee and liqueurs. Yet even that can't compare with actually making your own chocolates.

Formerly I would have agreed that the whole process was fiddly and time-consuming. However – after a lot of trial and error – I have discovered a quick and easy method of making deliciously light and smooth chocolates which, what's more, freeze extremely well for up to a month so can be made well in advance. Christmas is the time for treats, so I have included a couple of other ideas for homemade sweets – also with the thought that any of them would make very special Christmas gifts for special friends.

CRÈME *de* MENTHE JELLIES

·

MAKES APPROXIMATELY 48

These go down very well with coffee after a rich Christmas meal. To make them you need only buy a miniature bottle of crème de menthe liqueur, and oil of peppermint (available at most chemists), though a little expensive perhaps, does last for ages.

1 lb (450 g) granulated sugar	A few drops peppermint oil
¼ teaspoon cream of tartar	Green colouring
3½ oz (90 g) cornflour	
7½ oz (210 g) icing sugar	You will need a 7 inch (18 cm) square tin,
1¼ pints (750 ml) water	1¼ inch (3 cm) deep, buttered. A cake tin
1 level tablespoon golden syrup	will do if you don't have a shallow tin.
1 miniature bottle crème de menthe	

Put the sugar in a medium-sized pan with 5 fl oz (150 ml) of the water and heat very, very gently until all the sugar has dissolved. Then boil briskly to the 'soft-ball' stage (this is when the temperature reaches 240°F (115°C) – or, if you don't have a thermometer, it's when a little syrup dropped into cold water will just form a soft ball). But take it off the heat while you test it: it must not become hard toffee.

While the syrup is boiling, combine 7 oz (200 g) of the icing sugar and 3 oz (75 g) of the cornflour in another pan. Gradually stir in the remaining 1 pint (570 ml) of cold water, bring to the boil, then boil for 2 minutes. As soon as the sugar syrup reaches the soft-ball stage, pour it slowly (stirring constantly and protecting your hands from any splashes with a cloth) into the cornflour sauce. Sprinkle in the cream of tartar and boil very gently, stirring frequently, for about another 25 minutes or until the mixture is a very pale straw colour and semi-opaque.

Now remove the pan from the heat, beat in the golden syrup, crème de menthe and oil of peppermint (this last one is fairly potent stuff, so the best method is to insert a skewer into the oil, then allow a droplet to fall from the tip into the crème de menthe mixture). When you feel you have the correct peppermint flavour, add about 2 drops of green colouring, stir well and pour this mixture into the prepared tin. Then leave it overnight or until absolutely cold.

Finally combine the remaining cornflour and icing sugar. Tip the jelly out on to the mixture and cut into 1 inch (2.5 cm) strips. Roll these in the sugar mixture, cut across into 1 inch (2.5 cm) squares and leave on a rack to dry for several hours before packing into bags, boxes or jars along with some more coating (equal quantities of icing sugar and cornflour mixed).

BUTTERED TOFFEE BRAZILS

·

I always feel deprived if I don't get a box of buttered Brazils for Christmas – so to be on the safe side, I make my own! In fact I think they're nicer than any you can buy.

8 oz (225 g) Brazil nuts, shelled
3 oz (75 g) unsalted butter (unclarified weight), clarified
8 oz (225 g) soft dark brown sugar

You will need (believe it or not) a pair of well-scrubbed eyebrow tweezers and a lightly oiled plate.

First you need to clarify the butter and to do this you melt it in a small sauce-pan. When it has melted you can see the oil separate from the curd-like solids: carefully spoon this off for use, discarding the solids. An alternative way to do this is to start ahead of time and chill the melted butter in the refrigerator, whereupon the solids will sink to the bottom of their own accord, and the oily buttery part can be easily separated. (All this is for one reason: clarified butter burns less easily and so is good for toffee-making.)

Now place the clarified butter in a heavy-based saucepan then add the sugar and, keeping the heat no more than barely medium, wait until the sugar melts and begins to bubble. This needs very careful watching, so don't wander off. When the sugar has lost its grainy appearance and looks smooth, stir gently to incorporate the butter – if necessary remove from the heat to prevent it burn-ing. It is ready when the mixture looks like melted milk chocolate.

Next put the Brazil nuts, a few at a time, into the caramel and turn them over to coat them well. Have a lightly oiled plate ready, and use the tweezers to lift each one on to it (tweezers may sound like an odd utensil, but they do the job splendidly). When the toffee has set, place the nuts in little *petit four* cases and store in an airtight tin.

◆–◆–◆

Homemade truffles (see page 184).

HOMEMADE CHOCOLATE TRUFFLES

·

MAKES APPROXIMATELY 36

*T*his is a subject that experts get awfully fussed about and there are all kinds of rules and regulations about handling chocolate. This, in its pure sense, is not a subject to be grappling with amidst all the panics and pressures of Christmas. Therefore what I have on offer here are the easiest homemade truffles in the world. They will make an extra special gift for someone who is happy to consume them within 3 days and they make an equally special ending to any Christmas feast – served with liqueurs and coffee (see page 182).

Basic Truffle Mixture

5 oz (150 g) very best quality plain dessert chocolate

5 fl oz (150 ml) thick double cream

1 oz (25 g) unsalted butter

2 tablespoons rum or brandy

1 tablespoon Greek yoghurt

FOR THE PLAIN TRUFFLES:
1 dessertspoon cocoa powder

FOR THE GINGER TRUFFLES:
¾ oz (20 g) preserved ginger, very finely chopped, plus some extra cut into small pieces

FOR THE TOASTED ALMOND TRUFFLES:
1 oz (25 g) flaked almonds, very finely chopped and well toasted

FOR THE CHOCOLATE-COATED TRUFFLES:
2 oz (50 g) plain dessert chocolate and ½ teaspoon groundnut oil

You will need some paper sweet cases and (for the Chocolate-coated truffles) a sheet of silicone paper.

Break the chocolate into squares and place it in the bowl of a food processor. Switch on and grind the chocolate until it looks granular, like sugar. Now place the cream, butter and rum or brandy in a small saucepan and bring these to simmering point. Then, with the motor switched on, pour the mixture through the feeder tube of the processor and continue to blend until you have a smooth blended mixture. Now add the yoghurt and blend again for a few seconds. Next transfer the mixture, which will be very liquid at this stage, into a bowl, allow it to get quite cold, then cover it with cling film and refrigerate overnight. Don't worry: it *will* thicken up after several hours.

Next day divide the mixture equally between four small bowls, and keep each one in the refrigerator until you need it. Then proceed with the following to make four different varieties. Make sure you have all the little paper cases opened out ready before your hands get all chocolaty!

Plain Truffles

For these you simply sift 1 dessertspoon of cocoa powder on to a flat plate, then take heaped half teaspoons of the first batch of truffle mixture and either dust each one straightaway all over, which gives the truffle a rough rock-like appearance, *or* dust your hands in cocoa and roll each piece into a ball and then roll it into the cocoa powder if you like a smoother look. Place it immediately into a paper case. Obviously the less handling the better as the warmth of your hands melts the chocolate.

Ginger Truffles

Mix the finely chopped ginger into the second batch of truffle mixture using a fork, then proceed as above, taking small pieces, rolling or not (as you wish), and dusting with cocoa powder before transferring each one to a paper case.

Toasted Almond Truffles

Sprinkle the very finely chopped toasted almond flakes on a flat plate, take half a teaspoonful of the third batch of truffle mixture and roll it round in the nuts, pressing them to form an outer coating.

Chocolate-coated Truffles

For these you need to set the chocolate and oil in a bowl over some hot but not boiling water and allow it to melt until it becomes liquid, then remove the pan from the heat. Now spread some silicone paper on a flat surface and, dusting your hands with cocoa, roll each truffle into a little ball. Using two flat skewers, one to spike the truffle and one to manoeuvre it, dip each truffle in the chocolate so that it gets a thin coating and then quickly transfer it to the paper. If the chocolate begins to thicken replace the pan on the heat so that it will liquefy again. Leave the coated truffles to set completely, then, using a palette knife, quickly transfer them into their waiting paper cases.

Now arrange all the truffles in a box or boxes and cover. Keep them refrigerated and eat within 3 days. Alternatively, truffles are ideal for freezing.

◆-◆-◆

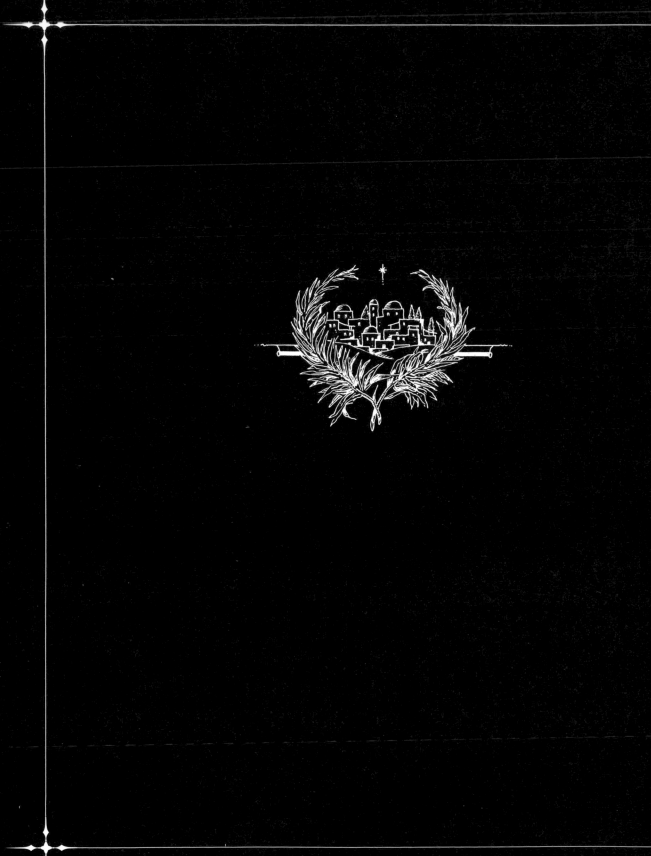

CHAPTER 11

THE
Last 36
Hours

What I hope to set out in this chapter is a kind of chronology of all that the cook needs to do in the final 36 hours leading up to Christmas lunch. Even if you're not serving the traditional lunch set out below, you may still find it helpful to see some sort of framework into which different recipes can be inserted.

First, a word of caution. On paper a detailed plan of action can look quite simple and straightforward – but plans on paper can easily lull us into a false sense of security. It's all very well congratulating yourself on having the food organised, but have you allowed for those last-minute panics that only Christmas can create?

I have encountered more than my share of distractions – like not being able to find a Christmas tree on Christmas Eve (except the very scrawniest) and wasting half the day in the search. One year when we did buy one early it wasn't too steady in its tub and a visiting dog contrived to topple it over, scattering lights and cherubs, earth and pine needles to every corner of the room.

Don't forget, too, that people drop in unexpectedly at Christmas. That's one of the lovely things about it, and you just have to accept that you might be taking off your apron and pouring drinks just when you thought you had space to make the mince pies! So, given the inevitable disruptions, this countdown is not a rigid, don't-forget-to-set-the-alarm-and-put-the-cat-out list of orders. It's a few gentle reminders to help you through some busy hours.

———◆·●·◆———

◆ CHRISTMAS EVE EARLY AM ◆
Last-minute Shopping

In practice this means sallying forth for the freshest vegetables (sprouts, leeks, parsnips, onions, carrots, celery, swede, potatoes) and fruit (oranges, tangerines, grapes, bananas, dates, cranberries), because they need to last over the whole holiday. Everyone else will be doing the same, of course, so do get out early to join the queues and, before you leave the house, read the various shopping lists (see pages 8–9) *out loud.* You may have forgotten something. Have you got any milk, cream, bread, pet food, the turkey . . . ?

◆ CHRISTMAS EVE MID-MORNING ◆
The Turkey Arrives

For my notes on frozen turkey see page 219, but let us assume your fresh and magnificent bird has reached its destination. There is no need to wash or wipe it, just place it on a sheet of greaseproof paper and remove the giblets. Make sure you know what it weighs: your supplier should have written it down – if not, you might find the bathroom scales helpful, but make sure you keep it on the greaseproof paper. Store it (uncovered) in the refrigerator till just before you go to bed. You may well need to remove one shelf from the refrigerator to house it, but if space is a desperate problem, don't worry: you can use an unheated bedroom, or the garage (with suitable covering) – even, in an emergency, the locked boot of the car which can be pretty cold on a winter's night.

GIBLET STOCK

However unpromising the giblets look, they make a wonderful stock for the turkey gravy and the meat from them will provide a splendid Christmas lunch for a deserving cat or dog.

The turkey giblets, including the neck and, if you're not using it for stuffing (see page 192), the liver
1 onion, sliced in half
1 carrot, sliced in half lengthways
A few parsley stalks
1 celery stalk (plus a few leaves)
1 bayleaf
6 whole black peppercorns
Salt
1½ pints (900 ml) water

First wash the giblets and put them in a saucepan with the halved onion, then cover with the water and bring up to simmering point. After removing any surface scum with a slotted spoon, add the remaining ingredients, half-cover the pan with a lid and simmer for 1½–2 hours. Then strain the stock and store, covered, in the refrigerator. I always think that it's when the giblet stock is simmering that you get the first fragrant aromas of Christmas lunch which fill you with the pleasure of anticipation!

— CHRISTMAS EVE LATER AM —
Preparing Vegetables

A good time to get these chores out of the way. Always my choice for Christmas lunch are the tiny, tight *button sprouts* and I prefer to serve them plain as there are so many other rich flavours around. Prepare 1½–2 lb (700 g–1 kg) for 8–10 people, and keep them stored in a polythene bag in the refrigerator till needed. Another regular is parsnips: my recipe for these is *Parmesan-baked parsnips* (see page 142). They can be prepared in advance right up to the oven-ready stage. Store them laid out on a tray in the refrigerator or a cool place. Also at this stage take the sausage rolls out of the freezer to defrost.

— CHRISTMAS EVE EARLY PM —
Make the Trifle

Christmas simply isn't Christmas without a trifle. I find this is the best time to assemble it. For the recipe see page 168.

— CHRISTMAS EVE 3 PM —
Carols and Baking

The tradition in our house is to see to all the Christmas baking to the backdrop of the *Festival of Nine Lessons and Carols* on BBC television from King's College, Cambridge. In the past I used to bake my *Sausage rolls* and *Mince pies* (pages 72 and 48) fresh at this time of the day, but in latter years I have taken to cooking them from the freezer. For me this is the moment when Christmas really begins: I always enjoy joining in the carols as the lovely aroma of Christmas baking wafts through the house (even if I do get a bit grumpy because I don't like the old translation of the scriptures that are not always read very well!).

For baking the mince pies from frozen, and the sausage rolls, which should be well defrosted, the oven needs to be pre-heated to gas mark 7, 425°F (220°C). Return the mince pies to their patty tins, brush them with milk and bake for 25–30 minutes. Then remove them to a wire rack to cool before dusting them with icing sugar and serving or storing in an airtight tin. The sausage rolls should be arranged on a greased baking sheet, brushed with beaten egg and baked at the above temperature for 20 minutes, then cooled on a rack.

NOTE: In fact sausage rolls are really best eaten freshly baked, so if there is no immediate call for them, take them from the freezer and cook as necessary.

Mistletoe and seasonal plants, Berwick Street market, London.

→ CHRISTMAS EVE LATER PM →
The Turkey Stuffing

Now is the time to make up the stuffing ready to go into the turkey tomorrow. I firmly believe that the whole idea of stuffing a large bird like a turkey is to help to counteract the drying-out process during cooking. Minced pork (or pork sausagemeat) is an ideal ingredient for this because the fatty juices from the pork help to keep the flesh of the turkey moist. For this reason all the stuffings below have pork as a main ingredient. All the stuffings are for a 12–14 lb (5.5–6.5 kg) turkey.

NOTE: If you like your stuffing firm, so that it cuts in slices, add a beaten egg to bind it. If, like me, you prefer it crumbly, leave the egg out.

EIGHTEENTH-CENTURY CHESTNUT STUFFING

This recipe is adapted from one I first came across in the cookery book written by the eighteenth-century writer, Hannah Glasse. Peeling chestnuts (see page 212) is a chore at the best of times, but with the pressures of Christmas it can seem even more tiresome. So, if you can get hold of peeled chestnuts in a vacuum pack or container, that will make life infinitely easier.

1 lb (450 g) peeled chestnuts, cooked and very finely chopped
1 large onion, finely chopped
The liver from the turkey, chopped small
4 oz (110 g) smoked streaky bacon, finely chopped
1 oz (25 g) butter
4 tablespoons chopped parsley
1 dessertspoon chopped fresh thyme
¼ teaspoon ground mace
8 oz (225 g) best quality pork sausagemeat, or finely minced pure pork
Salt and freshly milled black pepper

Melt the butter in a large frying-pan and cook the onion, bacon and chopped turkey liver for 10 minutes or so, until the onion looks transparent and everything is tinged gold at the edges. Now tip the contents of the pan into a large mixing bowl and add all the remaining ingredients. Season with salt and pepper, and mix very thoroughly.

TRADITIONAL PORK, SAGE AND ONION STUFFING

2 lb (1 kg) good quality pork sausagemeat or finely minced pure pork
4 heaped tablespoons white breadcrumbs
1 large onion, grated or very finely chopped
1 heaped dessertspoon dried sage
A little boiling water
1 egg, beaten (optional)
Salt and freshly milled black pepper

Combine the breadcrumbs with the onion and sage in a large mixing bowl, then stir in a little boiling water and mix thoroughly. Next work the sausagemeat into this mixture and season with salt and pepper. Leave the stuffing covered in a cool place – but not in the refrigerator, as it shouldn't be too cold when you come to stuff the turkey.

AMERICAN TURKEY STUFFING

This type of stuffing was first served to me at a delightful Thanksgiving Dinner given by some American friends. The recipe, as many are, was handed down from grandmother to mother to daughter. This is my own adaptation, which keeps the variety of flavours and textures (see page 194).

6 oz (175 g) white bread, cut into ½ inch (1 cm) cubes

8 oz (225 g) onions, chopped fairly small

4 sticks celery, cut into ½ inch (1 cm) chunks

1 lb (450 g) best quality thin pork sausages, skinned and sliced into ½ inch (1 cm) chunks

8 oz (225 g) Bramley apples, cored and chopped

4 oz (110 g) walnuts, chopped

2 oz (50 g) butter

1 dessertspoon chopped fresh thyme

The grated zest of 1 small lemon

½ teaspoon ground mace

Salt and freshly milled black pepper

Begin by melting the butter in a large frying-pan and lightly fry the chopped onions, celery and chunks of sausage until they become golden at the edges (this will take about 10 minutes). After that tip these into a large mixing bowl and add all the remaining ingredients. Mix very thoroughly, seasoning well.

← CHRISTMAS EVE EARLY EVENING →
Accompaniments

In our family there are those who like bread sauce as the accompaniment to turkey, and there are those who prefer cranberries. For the latter I always make the following sauce, one of the very nicest and one that can be made ahead without coming to any harm.

CRANBERRY AND ORANGE RELISH

SERVES 8 PEOPLE

1 lb (450 g) fresh cranberries

The rind and juice of 1 large orange

A 1½ inch (4 cm) piece cinnamon stick

4 cloves

1 heaped teaspoon freshly grated root ginger or ½ teaspoon ground ginger

3 oz (75 g) caster sugar

2–3 tablespoons port

Chop the cranberries in a food processor, or else press them through the fine blade of a mincer, then place them in a saucepan. Now pare off the coloured part of the orange rind with a potato peeler and cut it into very fine shreds. Add these, with the juice of the orange, to the pan followed by the ginger, sugar and spices. Bring everything up to simmering point, stir well, put a lid on the pan and let it all simmer very gently for about 5 minutes. Then remove the pan from the heat, stir in the port and, when it has cooled, pour into a serving dish. Cover with cling film and keep in a cool place till needed. Don't forget to remove the cloves and cinnamon before serving!

Get Ahead!

If you're still on your feet by this time, you can also prepare the onion and cloves ready for the *Traditional bread sauce* (see page 197) and place in a saucepan covered with cling film. And why not weigh out the butter and sugar for the *Christmas rum sauce* (see page 199) and cover them in a saucepan ready for the off tomorrow?

✦ CHRISTMAS EVE BEFORE YOU GO TO BED ✦

In my younger days I used to dash off to Midnight Mass and return home with a group of friends for spiced cider, sausage rolls and pickled onions at about 1.30. Nowadays I like a good night's sleep before cooking the Christmas lunch, so I opt for an early night and morning Mass instead. Early or late, though, it is important to *take the turkey out of the fridge* now to allow it to come to room temperature so that it heats up immediately you put it in the oven. The same applies to the stuffing, and you also need to remove 6 oz (175 g) of butter to soften ready for the morning. Now your refrigerator will be looking on the empty side, so it's a good time to slip in the white wine, champagne, mineral water, children's drinks and anything else that needs to be chilled.

✦ CHRISTMAS DAY EARLY AM ✦
What Time is Lunch?

The specific timings that follow are those tested over the years in our house, but because lunch time will vary from one family to another you can adjust these timings to suit yourself. With young children you will doubtless be up early and want to eat lunch reasonably early; with older children it's not quite so important to open the presents at the first light of dawn!

For an average family-sized 14 lb (6.5 kg) turkey (oven-ready weight) I am calculating for a 2.00 pm lunch. If you plan to eat half an hour later or earlier, simply add or subtract 30 minutes to or from my timings.

American stuffing (see page 193).

Principles of Turkey Cooking

Many people have their own favourite way to cook turkey, usually because it's the way they were taught. I'm sure there is no best way, and I offer you the following method simply because it has always worked well for me and countless others. The turkey is placed in a 'tent' of foil, which essentially means it cooks in an oven within an oven. If you wrap the foil too closely to the turkey, though, it ends up steaming instead of roasting. Give it plenty of space between the flesh and the foil and it will roast in its own buttery juices without becoming dry. This method keeps all the juices intact. If you allow the bird to relax for 30–45 minutes before carving all the juices which have bubbled up to the surface will seep back and ensure the meat is moist and succulent (see page 198).

➤ CHRISTMAS DAY 7.45 AM ➤

Pre-heat the oven to gas mark 7, 425°F (220°C)

TRADITIONAL ROAST TURKEY

For a 14 lb (6.5 kg) turkey. See page 219 for timings for other weights of turkey.

1 × 14 lb (6.5 kg) turkey, oven-ready
6 oz (175 g) butter, softened
8 oz (225 g) very fat streaky bacon
Salt and freshly milled black pepper
1 quantity of stuffing (see page 192–3)

You will also need extra-wide turkey foil.

First stuff the turkey with your chosen stuffing. Loosen the skin with your hands and pack the stuffing into the neck end, pushing it up between the flesh and the skin towards the breast (not too tightly, because it will expand during the cooking). Press it in gently to make a nicely rounded end, then tuck the neck flap under the bird's back and secure with a small skewer. Don't expect to get all the stuffing in this end – put the rest into the body cavity.

NOTE: It is only dangerous to put turkey stuffing inside the body cavity if either the turkey or the stuffing is not defrosted properly, because the heat will not penetrate it quickly enough. If both are at room temperature it is perfectly safe.

Now arrange two large sheets of foil across your roasting tin, one widthways and the other lengthways (no need to butter them). Lay the turkey on its back in the centre then rub it generously all over with the butter, making sure the thigh bones are particularly well covered. Next season the bird all over with salt and pepper, and lay the bacon over the breast with the rashers overlapping each other.

Now wrap the turkey loosely in the foil: the parcel must be firmly sealed but roomy enough to provide an air space around most of the upper part of the bird. So bring one piece of foil up and fold both ends over to make a pleat along the length of the breast-bone. Then bring the other piece up at both ends and crimp and fold to make a neat parcel.

◆ CHRISTMAS DAY 8.15 AM ◆

Place the turkey in the pre-heated oven, where it will cook at the initial high temperature for 40 minutes.

Once it is in, you can peel the potatoes ready for roasting and keep them covered with cold water in a saucepan. Now begin making the bread sauce.

TRADITIONAL BREAD SAUCE

SERVES 8 PEOPLE

4 oz freshly made white breadcrumbs (a 2-day-old white loaf with crusts removed will be hard enough to grate, but the best way is in a liquidiser, if you have one)
1 large onion
15–18 whole cloves or grated nutmeg
1 bayleaf
8 black peppercorns
1 pint (570 ml) creamy milk
2 oz (50 g) butter
2 tablespoons double cream
Salt and freshly milled black pepper

Cut the onion in half and stick the cloves in it (how many you use is a personal matter – I happen to like a pronounced flavour of cloves). If you don't like them at all, you can use some freshly grated nutmeg instead. Place the onion studded with cloves, plus the bayleaf and the peppercorns in a saucepan together with the milk. Add some salt, then bring everything up to boiling point. Take off the heat, cover the pan and leave in a warm place for the milk to infuse for 2 hours or more.

When you're ready to make the sauce (see page 199), remove the onion, bayleaf and peppercorns and keep them on one side. Stir the breadcrumbs into the milk and add 1 oz (25 g) of the butter. Leave the saucepan on a very low heat, stirring now and then, until the crumbs have swollen and thickened the sauce – approximately 15 minutes. Now replace the clove-studded onion and again leave the pan in a warm place till the sauce is needed. Just before serving, remove the onion and spices. Reheat gently, then beat in the remaining butter and the cream and taste to check the seasoning. Pour into a warm serving jug and stand until needed.

◆ CHRISTMAS DAY 8.55 AM ◆

Lower the oven temperature to gas mark 3, 325°F (170°C). *Now take a break!* At this point everything should be under control so you can take time out of the kitchen to help the kids unwrap their presents, have a coffee or tidy the house. After that prepare and set the lunch table, making sure you have all the right glasses for pre-lunch drinks as well as the table. It's a good idea to arrange the coffee tray now, too, and line up the brandy and liqueur glasses. Pop the plates and serving-dishes into the warming oven, and don't forget to warm a large plate for the turkey.

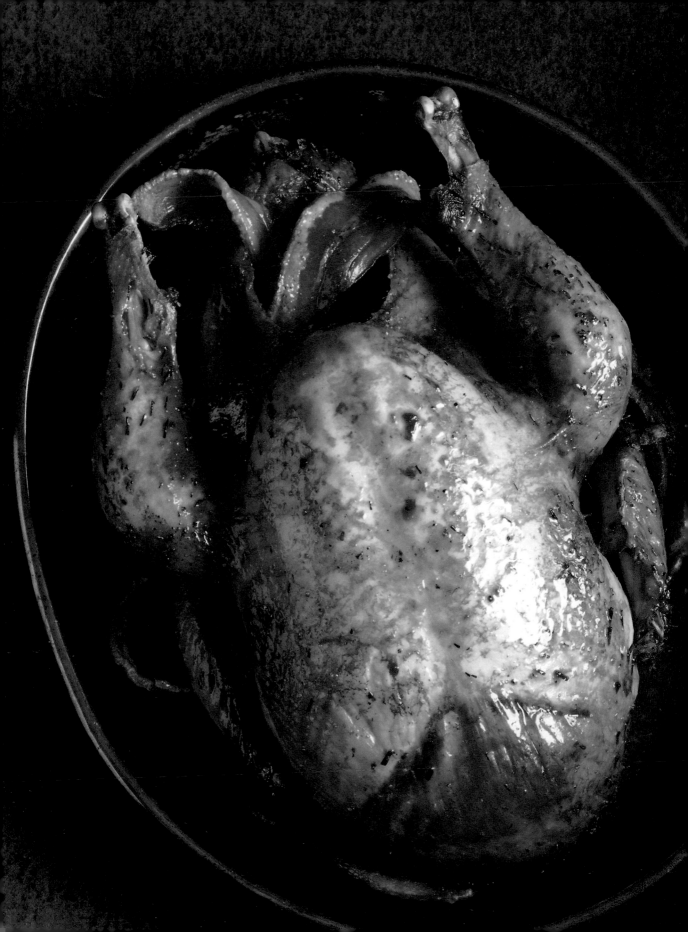

✦ CHRISTMAS DAY 11.30 AM ✦

If you're going to serve *bacon rolls* and/or *chipolatas* now is the time to prepare them, as follows: brush a shallow baking sheet with oil and arrange the sausages on it in two rows. For the bacon, stretch the rinded rashers out as far as you can, then roll them up very tightly, thread them on to long flat skewers and place them next to the chipolatas, ready to go into the oven later.

✦ CHRISTMAS DAY 11.45 AM ✦

Now is the time to finish off the *bread sauce*. Place it in a jug with some butter to melt over the surface, and keep it in a warm place.

✦ CHRISTMAS DAY 12.00 NOON ✦

Fill a saucepan quite full with boiling water, put it on the heat and, when it comes back to the boil, place a steamer on top of the pan and turn it down to a gentle simmer. Put the Christmas pudding in the steamer, cover and leave to steam away until 2.15 pm. You'll need to check the water from time to time and maybe top it up a bit.

✦ CHRISTMAS DAY 12.15 PM ✦

The Christmas pudding brings us, naturally enough, to the *rum sauce* whose time has now come. Make it as follows:

CHRISTMAS RUM SAUCE

SERVES 8 PEOPLE

3 oz (75 g) butter
2½ oz (60 g) plain flour
1 pint (570 ml) creamy milk
2 oz (50 g) caster sugar
3 (or more) tablespoons dark rum
1 tablespoon double cream

Place 2½ oz (60 g) of the butter in a saucepan with 2½ oz (60 g) flour, pour in the milk, then, using a balloon whisk, whisk everything vigorously together over a medium heat. As soon as it comes to simmering point and has thickened, turn the heat right down to its lowest setting, stir in the sugar and let the sauce cook for 10 minutes. After that add the rum, the remaining ½ oz (15 g) butter and 1 tablespoon cream. Pour the hot sauce into a jug, then cover the surface with clingfilm and keep warm until required.

Traditional roast turkey (see page 196).

⟶ CHRISTMAS DAY 12.30 PM ⟵

Increase the oven temperature to gas mark 6, 400°F (200°C). Now get some help, because you've got to get the turkey out of the oven and it's heavy! Remove the foil from the top and sides of the bird, and take off the bacon slices. Now baste the turkey very thoroughly with a long-handled spoon, then return it to the oven for a further 30–45 minutes to finish browning – give it as much basting as you can during this final cooking period. The bacon rashers can be placed on a heat-proof plate and put back in the oven to finish cooking till all the fat has melted and there are just very crisp bits left. (I like to serve these crunchy bits with the turkey as well as bacon rolls!)

⟶ CHRISTMAS DAY 12.45 PM ⟵

After you've dealt with the turkey, par-boil the potatoes for 10 minutes then drain them. Put the lid back on the saucepan, and shake the potatoes quite heftily in the saucepan so that they become fluffy round the edges. Now take a solid roasting tin, add 2 oz (50 g) lard to it, and place on direct heat to let the fat melt and begin to sizzle. When it is really hot, add the potatoes and (using an oven glove to protect your hands) tip the tin and baste the potatoes so all are coated with fat. Then place the roasting tin in the oven with the turkey.

⟶ CHRISTMAS DAY 1.00 PM ⟵

Now for the parsnips. Take another roasting tin and add 3 tablespoons of oil and 1 tablespoon of butter to it and place over direct heat. When the butter and oil are hot, add the parsnips and baste them in the same way as the potatoes. By now it will be time for the turkey to come out of the oven.

⟶ CHRISTMAS DAY 1.15 PM ⟵

Remove the turkey from the oven and increase the temperature to gas mark 8, 450°F (230°C). Place the parsnips on the middle shelf of the oven (with the potatoes on the top), and the chipolatas on the lowest shelf or floor of the oven.

Transfer the turkey to a warm serving plate: it will be fine left to relax in the kitchen temperature for up to 50 minutes loosely covered with double foil without losing its heat. Next pour the giblet stock into a pan and allow it to heat up gently. Tip the turkey fat from the foil into the tin, discard the foil, then spoon off all the excess fat from the roasting tin into a bowl. This fat is *precious*: it's wonderful for sautéeing potatoes, and have you ever tried turkey jelly and dripping spread on hot slices of toast and sprinkled with salt and pepper? A wonderful Boxing Day breakfast treat!

Next make the giblet gravy. When you have spooned off the excess fat from the roasting tin and only the dark juices are left, work about 2 level tablespoons flour into these juices over a low heat. Now, using a balloon whisk, whisk in the giblet stock, bit by bit, until you have a smooth gravy. Let it bubble and reduce a little to concentrate the flavour, and taste and season with salt and pepper. Then pour into a jug and keep warm.

━━━━━ CHRISTMAS DAY 1.30 PM ━━━━━

Turn the chipolatas and bacon rolls over, then you are free for a few minutes to go and have a pre-lunch glass of champagne. You deserve it.

━━━━━ CHRISTMAS DAY 1.45 PM ━━━━━

Pour boiling water over the sprouts, add salt and leave to boil for 5–6 minutes, then drain in a colander. While the sprouts are cooking, summon the carver and get all hands on deck to help dish up. And don't forget that lovely stuffing inside the turkey!

━━━━━ CHRISTMAS DAY 2.00 PM ━━━━━

Lunch is served. *Bon appetit!*

━━━━━ CHRISTMAS DAY (A LITTLE LATER) ━━━━━

Remove the pudding from the steamer and take off the wrapping. Slide a palette knife all round the pudding, then turn it out on to a warmed plate. Place a suitably sized sprig of holly on top. Now warm a ladleful of brandy over direct heat, and as soon as the brandy is hot ask someone to set light to it. Place the ladle, now gently flaming, on top of the pudding – but don't pour it over until you reach the table. When you do, pour it slowly over the pudding, sides and all, and watch it flame to the cheers of the assembled company! When both flames and cheers have died down, serve the pudding with rum sauce, or rum or brandy butter.

A very important message for all frazzled Christmas cooks. The good news is that what you now have, in addition to your aching limbs and heavy eyelids, is a house full of food and absolutely no more cooking to do. So stretch out, fill your glass and have a very Happy Christmas!

━━━◆━●━◆━━━

CHAPTER 12

Supper Dishes
AND
Left-overs

*I*t is one of the poignant pleasures of Christmas that, once the lunch is over and the last of the washing-up taken care of, for the next few days I do not have to think about food. After all, the house is stuffed with it: no one's yet touched the trifle or the cake, there arc tins of mince pies and sausage rolls, there is cold ham, turkey, cheese, fruit, nuts, dates . . .

Then, probably about three days later, I begin to feel like cooking something! So this chapter has two purposes really. First it is about using up all the last scraps – of turkey, ham, vegetables, cheese and so on – and utilising the turkey carcase or ham bone to make a wonderful stock for soups. But it also aims to offer a few ideas for those homely dishes that can be so welcome after the excesses of the festival: after all that emphasis on meat or game, for instance, what could be nicer than superlative scrambled eggs flavoured with a few strips of smoked salmon, or what more beautiful supper dish than an Omelette Arnold Bennett could there be for those who feel ever so slightly jaded by Christmas fare?

CREAMED TURKEY *en* CROÛTE

·

SERVES 6 PEOPLE

This really is something of a moveable feast: if you have left-over ham, that can be used instead of bacon, leeks can replace the onion, celery the mushrooms and so on. But given that I must say that turkey in a cream sauce wrapped in a sort of blanket of crisp flaky pastry is something quite special.

12 oz (350 g) cooked turkey, chopped	3 fl oz (75 ml) cream – single or double, whatever's left
3 oz (75 g) smoked bacon, finely chopped	1 tablespoon chopped fresh parsley
1 oz (25 g) butter	Salt and freshly milled black pepper
1 medium onion, chopped	1 quantity Quick flaky pastry (see page 72)
3 oz (75 g) mushrooms, quartered	or 12 oz (350 g) frozen puff pastry, thawed
1 oz (25 g) plain flour	Beaten egg to glaze
12 fl oz (350 ml) turkey stock (from the carcase, see page 208)	You will need a baking sheet, greased.
2 tablespoons brandy	

PRE-HEAT THE OVEN TO GAS MARK 7, 425°F (220°C)

First of all melt the butter in a large saucepan and gently sauté the onion in it for 5 minutes, then add the mushrooms and let these soften a bit, keeping them on the move, for a further 5 minutes. After that remove the onion and mushrooms to a plate with a draining spoon. Next add the bacon to the pan and fry it till it turns a pale gold at the edges, at which point return the mushrooms and onion (and any juices) then sprinkle in the flour. Stir till the flour has soaked up all the buttery juices and ignore its unpromising appearance.

Next add the stock, little by little, still stirring until you have a smooth thick sauce. Lastly add the parsley, cream and brandy. Season to taste. Remove the pan from the heat and let the mixture cool.

When you are ready to cook the pie, roll out the pastry to a 12 inch (30 cm) square, trimming if necessary. Lift the square on to a greased baking sheet. Now mix the turkey pieces into the cold sauce, then place this mixture in the centre of the pastry. Glaze round the edge of the pastry with beaten egg, then pull the opposite corners of the pastry to the centre and pinch all the edges firmly together, so you have a square with pinched edges in the shape of an X. Glaze all over with beaten egg and decorate with any pastry trimming. Glaze these too and then bake the pie for about 30 minutes or until the pastry is well risen and golden. Serve the pie cut into squares with a plain green salad.

GOOSE *(pheasant or duck)* GIBLET STOCK

.

I t is perfectly all right to use duck or pheasant giblets instead of goose giblets in this recipe, although you will only need 1 pint (570 ml) water if you do.

The giblets and neck of the goose	1 bayleaf
1 onion, sliced in half	1 sprig thyme
1 carrot, split lengthways	6 black peppercorns
1 thick celery stick, cut into chunks (plus leaves)	1½ pints (900 ml) water
	Salt

Wash the neck and giblets then place tnem in a medium-sized saucepan and add the rest of the ingredients along with the water. Bring everything up to the boil, skim off any scum that rises to the surface, then turn thc heat down to a gentle simmer. Put a lid half on the pan and simmer for 1½–2 hours. After that strain the stock, and bring back up to simmering point before making gravy.

◆ ◆ ◆

HAM BONE STOCK

.

The bones and scraps of a ham	A few parsley stalks
2 celery sticks (plus leaves)	1 bayleaf
1 large carrot, split lengthways	1 sprig thyme
1 leek, split lengthways	4 pints (2.25 litres) cold water
6 black peppercorns	

Place all the ingredients in a cooking pot and add the cold water. Bring everything up to simmering point, remove any scum from the surface and simmer gently (covered) for 1½–2 hours.

◆ ◆ ◆

VEGETABLE STOCK

·

1 stick celery, cut in half and split lengthways	12 black peppercorns
2 small carrots, split in half lengthways	2 bayleaves
2 small onions, sliced	Salt
Parsley stalks and celery leaves	1–1½ pints (570–900 ml) cold water

Simply place all the ingredients in a saucepan, cover it with a lid, bring everything to the boil, and boil briskly for 30 minutes. After that strain, discarding the vegetables, and the stock is ready for use.

◆—◆—◆

QUICK BLENDER HOLLANDAISE

·

SERVES 4 PEOPLE

6 oz (175 g) butter	3 large egg yolks
1 tablespoon wine vinegar	A pinch of salt
2 tablespoons lemon juice	

Put the butter into a small saucepan and allow it to melt slowly. Place the wine and lemon juice in another pan and bring these to the boil. Meanwhile blend the egg yolks in a liquidiser or food processor, then – with the motor still switched on – gradually add the hot lemon and vinegar.

When the butter reaches the boil, start to pour this in very slowly in a thin trickle (with the motor running all the time) till it is all is added and the sauce is thickened. To keep the sauce warm, place it in a basin over some hot water till ready to use.

◆—◆—◆

TURKEY SOUP

·

*F*ew of us nowadays have time in our lives to make real homemade soups with proper stock. But Christmas does provide a rare opportunity, and it can provide quite a therapeutic exercise after the pressures of pre-Christmas.

FOR THE STOCK:	FOR THE SOUP:
1 turkey carcase (including the skin and debris, like bits of stuffing)	1 lb (450 g) vegetables (any combination of carrots, leeks, swede, celery and onions) chopped, per 1 pint (570 ml) turkey stock
1 carrot, split lengthways	
1 onion, cut in half	1 heaped teaspoon turkey dripping or butter per 1 lb (450 g) vegetables
2 celery sticks, cut into chunks	
2 sprigs thyme	Salt and freshly milled black pepper
2 bayleaves	
12 black peppercorns	
Salt	

To make the stock, take your largest cooking pot and break the turkey carcase into it (along with all the bits that cling to it), then add the rest of the ingredients. Cover with water, bring up to simmering point, skim off any scum that rises to the surface, then simmer for 2 hours. After that strain the stock and discard all the debris.

For the soup, sweat the chopped vegetables in dripping or butter in a large pan (lid on) for 10 minutes over a low heat. Measure in the stock and leave to simmer, again with the lid on, very gently for 1½ hours. After that purée the soup either in a food processor or liquidiser, or through a sieve. Taste to check the seasoning, and re-heat before serving.

NOTE: 1 pint (570 ml) stock and 1 lb (450 g) vegetables will make enough soup for 4 people.

STILTON SOUP *with* PARMESAN CROÛTONS

·

SERVES 4 TO 6 PEOPLE

*N*ot simply a recipe for left-over bits of Stilton, this one, but a delicious creamy soup that can enhance any dinner or supper party (see page 210).

2 oz (50 g) butter	1 tablespoon double cream
1 onion, finely chopped	Salt and freshly milled black pepper
1 leek, cleaned and chopped	
1 large potato, diced small	FOR THE CROÛTONS:
1 heaped tablespoon plain flour	8 oz (225 g) stale bread, cut into small
1 pint (570 ml) chicken stock	cubes
5 fl oz (150 ml) dry cider	4 dessertspoons freshly grated Parmesan
4 oz (110 g) Stilton cheese, grated	cheese
10 fl oz (275 ml) milk	4 tablespoons oil

Start off by melting the butter in a thick-based saucepan, then add the prepared vegetables and some salt, and cook gently with the lid on for 5–10 minutes to draw out the juices. Next stir in the flour to absorb the juices and, when smooth, gradually pour in the cider – still stirring. Now add the chicken stock, cover the pan and simmer *gently* for 30 minutes. After that, add the milk and Stilton and re-heat, stirring, until the cheese has melted and the soup is just below boiling point. Taste and season with salt and pepper, then stir in the cream. At this stage you can purée the soup in a food processor or else press it through a sieve; or, if you prefer the texture of the chopped vegetables, keep it as it is. Serve the soup with Parmesan croûtons.

For the croûtons, pre-heat the oven to gas mark 4, 350°F (180°C), or preheat the grill. Place the bread cubes in a bowl, sprinkle in the oil, then stir them around till the bread has soaked up all the oil. Next add the freshly grated Parmesan, and stir again till all the bread cubes are well coated. Spread them out over a baking sheet and either bake in a pre-heated oven for 10 minutes, or else place them under a pre-heated grill, turning as necessary. (If you use the grill, watch them like a hawk as they can burn very easily.) These croûtons can be made well in advance and stored in an airtight tin for up to 2 weeks.

NOTE: Be careful not to boil the soup when re-heating.

◆─◆─◆

HAM HASH CAKES *with* PARSLEY SAUCE

·

SERVES 4 TO 6 PEOPLE

If you don't want to make parsley sauce these are good served with some pickled dill cucumbers and sharp mustard, or else with the Spiced apricot and orange or Christmas chutney (see pages 60 and 61).

12 oz (350 g) cooked ham, cut into chunks	Freshly milled black pepper
1 onion, quartered	
8 oz (225 g) boiled potatoes (cooked weight)	FOR THE PARSLEY SAUCE:
	15 fl oz (425 ml) milk
1 egg, size 1	1 tablespoon single cream
1 tablespoon chopped gherkins	1½ (40 g) butter
1 tablespoon chopped parsley	¾ oz (20 g) plain flour
2 oz (50 g) fine breadcrumbs	3 tablespoons finely chopped parsley
1 tablespoon butter	1 teaspoon lemon juice
1 tablespoon oil	Salt and freshly milled black pepper

If you have a food processor this couldn't be simpler: just put the ham, onion, potatoes, egg and parsley in the goblet and blend till the ham is shredded quite finely. Alternatively you could use a conventional mincer, with the coarse blade fitted.

Transfer the mixture to a bowl, stir in the chopped gherkins and taste and season with freshly milled pepper, but probably not salt. Now divide the mixture into eight equal portions, shape them into neat rounds and press a light coating of breadcrumbs over each one. Then chill the hash cakes in the refrigerator till needed. To cook them, melt the butter with the oil in a frying-pan and fry the cakes till golden and crisp – which will take about 5–8 minutes on each side.

To make the parsley sauce, place the first four ingredients in a saucepan and whisk them over the heat till smooth and thickened. Then cook for 5 minutes before adding the parsley and lemon juice, and season to taste.

NOTE: For extra flavour you can infuse the milk with the parsley stalks first – but let it get absolutely cold before using it with this method.

◆━◆

Stilton soup with Parmesan croûtons (see page 209).

CHESTNUT SOUP *with* BACON *and* THYME CROÛTONS

·

SERVES 4 PEOPLE

A bone from a baked ham makes a superlative stock for a number of soups (such as lentil or split pea), but it helps to make the very best chestnut soup of all.

8 oz (225 g) peeled chestnuts (see opposite) – approximately 1 lb (450 g) unpeeled weight	FOR THE CROÛTONS: 4 oz (110 g) stale white bread, cut into small cubes
1 stick celery, chopped	4 tablespoons olive oil
1 small onion, chopped	1 rasher bacon, very finely chopped
1 small carrot, chopped	½ teaspoon finely chopped fresh thyme leaves
2 pints (1.2 litres) ham stock (see page 206)	
Salt and freshly milled pepper	

To make the soup, you simply place all the ingredients in a large saucepan, season discreetly with salt and pepper, bring up to simmering point, then put a lid on and simmer very gently for 45 minutes.

While that's happening you can prepare the croûtons. Heat the oil in a large frying-pan and cook the bacon gently for 5 minutes, then turn the heat up to its highest setting, add the cubes of bread together with the thyme, and toss them around (keeping them constantly on the move) until they, and the bacon, have turned a deep golden-brown colour and become very crisp and crunchy.

Turn them out on to some absorbent kitchen paper. Then, as soon as the soup is ready, transfer it to a blender and purée until smooth. Re-heat it in the rinsed-out pan and serve in warmed soup bowls, with the croûtons, bacon and thyme sprinkled over.

Peeling Chestnuts

Not a particularly easy job this, but the best method I have come across is as follows: rinse the chestnuts, then make a small incision in the flat side of the shell of each nut. Place them in a saucepan with cold water to cover, bring to the boil and boil gently for 10 minutes or so. Take the pan off the heat and use a draining spoon to remove the chestnuts from the water two or three at a time.

Peel these before removing the next batch. Take care to remove the inner skin from the crevices in the chestnuts – you will have to break the nut apart to do so, but for making a soup this won't matter.

SCRAMBLED EGGS *with* SMOKED SALMON

·

SERVES 2 PEOPLE

*I*f you were lucky enough to buy (or receive) a side of smoked salmon for Christmas, then you'll be bound to have lots of little pieces left over. Although this is one of the simplest dishes in the world, Scrambled eggs with smoked salmon never fails to please.

4 large eggs	2 oz (50 g) butter
4 oz (110 g) smoked salmon	Salt and freshly milled black pepper
4 tablespoons milk	

First of all the smoked salmon needs to be chopped up fairly small, then put in a jug or mug. Pour the milk over it, stir well so that all the fish gets a good coating of milk, then leave aside to soak for 20 minutes or so. After that melt half the butter in a small heavy-based saucepan on a lowish heat, and meanwhile break the eggs into a bowl, season them with salt and pepper and beat them well.

When the butter is foaming swirl it round the sides of the pan and pour in the beaten eggs. Take a wooden spoon and stir constantly – making sure you get right into the corner of the saucepan. When the eggs have just begun to solidify but there is still a fair amount of liquid, add the smoked salmon pieces (plus any milk which they have not absorbed) and keep stirring continuously. When almost all the liquid has gone, remove the pan from the heat, add the rest of the butter and continue stirring – the eggs will finish cooking to a creamy mass in the heat of the pan. Serve straightaway on triangles of fried bread or simply with slices of brown bread and butter.

◆━●━◆

TURKEY FLAN *with* LEEKS *and* CHEESE

·

SERVES 6 TO 8 PEOPLE

*T*his can be made with a combination of left-over turkey or chicken and pieces of cheese. You could also add some chopped pieces of ham if there is some left over. Having said that, I think this tastes so good that at other times of the year it is worth cooking some chicken specially to make it! Serve the flan warm with a tossed crisp green salad.

FOR THE CHEESE PASTRY:
6 oz (175 g) self-raising flour
3 oz (75 g) butter
2 oz (50 g) Cheddar cheese, grated
½ teaspoon mustard powder
Salt and freshly milled black pepper
Cold water to mix

FOR THE FILLING:
10–12 oz (275–350 g) cooked turkey, chicken or ham (or a mixture), thinly sliced
1 lb (450 g) leeks, washed thoroughly and sliced

1½ oz (40 g) plus 1 teaspoon butter
15 fl oz (425 ml) creamy milk or a mixture of milk and left-over cream
3 oz (75 g) cheese, grated
1 oz (25 g) plain flour
Salt and freshly milled black pepper
A little freshly grated nutmeg
1 egg, size 1, beaten
Cayenne pepper

You will need a 10 inch (25 cm) quiche tin.

PRE-HEAT THE OVEN TO GAS MARK 5, 375°F (190°C)
AND POP IN A HEAVY BAKING SHEET TO PRE-HEAT

First make up the pastry by rubbing the flour into the butter till crumbly, then add the cheese, mustard and seasoning together with just enough cold water to make a dough that leaves the bowl clean. Place the dough in a polythene bag and leave to rest in the refrigerator for 20 minutes or so.

Meanwhile melt the teaspoon of butter in a frying-pan, swirl it round the pan and then, keeping the heat low, add the leeks and let them gently cook for about 6 minutes and exude some of their juice. After that place the leeks in a sieve, strain off any juices into a bowl and set aside.

Next roll out the pastry and use it to line the prepared pie tin. Prick the base of the pastry with a fork, then pre-bake on the centre shelf of the oven for 15 minutes.

While that's happening put the 1½ oz (40 g) butter, milk and flour in a sauce-

214

pan and bring up to the boil, whisking all the time, until you have a smooth thick sauce. Season with salt, pepper and a little nutmeg, then leave the sauce to simmer gently for 5 minutes. Remove the pastry case from the oven and arrange the leeks over the base, followed by the slices of turkey, chicken or ham.

Now pour the reserved leek juice into the sauce, add three-quarters of the grated cheese and the beaten egg and mix well. Pour the sauce evenly over the contents of the flan and sprinkle the remaining cheese on top together with a dusting of cayenne. Bake the flan at the same temperature as above on the baking sheet for 25–30 minutes or until nicely browned on top.

—◆—●—◆—

POTTED CHEESE

·

SERVES 6 TO 8 PEOPLE

This can be made with leftover Stilton, Cheddar or – best of all – with Cheshire cheese. Serve it in little ramekins with celery, a bowl of assorted nuts (with plenty of nutcrackers), a few muscatel raisins and some really good port.

8 oz (225 g) cheese (as above)	¼ teaspoon ground mace
4 oz (110 g) butter, softened	½ teaspoon mustard powder
1½ fl oz (40 ml) sherry	Salt and freshly milled black pepper

Grate the cheese into a mixing bowl, then add the rest of the ingredients. Now beat it all together like mad until you have a very fluffy, smooth paste (an electric hand whisk will save you a lot of energy). Taste and season as required with salt and pepper, then pack the mixture into an earthenware pot or soufflé dish, or else into eight ramekin dishes. Leave the potted cheese in a cool place (though not in the refrigerator) until ready to serve. Serve with cheese crackers or oat biscuits. It is also good spread on toast or toasted under the grill till brown and bubbling.

—◆—●—◆—

OMELETTE ARNOLD BENNETT

·

SERVES 4 PEOPLE AS A LUNCH OR 8 AS A FIRST COURSE

At London's Savoy Hotel they have had this omelette on the menu for generations. It is a truly great recipe, and here I offer my version of the original. We always make this recipe whenever there is some leftover hollandaise in the fridge.

5 eggs, size 1	1 oz (25 g) Gruyère cheese, grated
6 oz (175 g) smoked haddock, Finnan haddock if possible	1 rounded tablespoon grated Parmesan cheese
6 fl oz (175 ml) creamy milk	
1 bayleaf	**TO SERVE:**
Salt and freshly milled black pepper	Watercress
½ oz (15 g) plain flour	Olive oil
1 oz (25 g) butter	Coarsely crushed rock salt
2 tablespoon Quick blender hollandaise (see page 207)	
	You will need a 10 inch (25 cm) frying-pan.

Start off by poaching the haddock in the milk in a medium saucepan. Add some freshly milled black pepper and a bayleaf but don't add salt yet because there's usually quite a bit in the haddock. It will take about 10 minutes to cook, depending on the thickness. After that remove it from the heat and strain off all the cooking liquid into a jug – press the fish to squeeze out every last drop of juice. Then remove the skin and bone and flake the flesh or chop it into fairly small pieces.

The next thing is to make up a sauce. Melt ½ oz (15 g) of the butter in a medium-sized saucepan, stir in the flour and then gradually whisk in the fish cooking liquid bit by bit until it is all incorporated and you have a smooth glossy sauce. Turn the heat very low and leave the sauce to just about bubble for 5 minutes, then add half the chopped fish together with the hollandaise. Everything up to this stage (provided you place some cling film over the fish sauce to prevent a skin forming) can be done well in advance.

Then, when you are ready to make the omelette, pre-heat the grill to the highest setting. Beat the eggs and add the rest of the chopped haddock and a little salt. Now melt the remaining ½ oz (15 g) butter in the frying-pan and when it's hot and foaming pour in the eggs. After 2 minutes, begin to draw the edges into the centre, tilting the pan to let all the liquid egg run into the gaps. When you feel half the egg has set turn the heat down and start to spoon the sauce mixture evenly all over the egg, using a palette knife to spread it out.

You'll need to be pretty nifty with this bit. Now sprinkle the Gruyère and Parmesan cheeses over the surface and place the omelette under the grill approximately 5 inches (13 cm) from the heat for 2 minutes until it has set but not browned at all. It's very important to keep everything creamy and moist. It will be quite puffy and golden at the edges, so now remove it from the heat and leave it to relax in the frying-pan in a warm place for about 10 minutes. This relaxing process is important if you want to serve it as a first course, because it will ensure you can cut it easily into portions. Serve them garnished with generous bunches of watercress that have been sprinkled with a minute amount of olive oil and some coarsely crushed rock salt.

COMPOTE *of* FIGS *in* PORT

·

SERVES 4 PEOPLE

*D*essert figs that have become too dry to eat as they are can be excellent made into a compote. This is superb served with Prune ice cream (see page 173), but failing that, try it with some Greek yoghurt.

8 oz (225 g) whole dried figs (no-soak, or else soaked overnight and drained)	2 whole almonds
10 fl oz (275 ml) water	The grated zest and juice of 1 orange
2 oz (50 g) demerara sugar	3 fl oz (75 ml) port

PRE-HEAT THE OVEN TO GAS MARK 2, 300°F (150°C)

Cook the figs in the same way as the Compote of prunes in port (see page 173).

When they're cooked, add the juice of the orange and the port, then arrange them in a glass serving dish and serve well chilled.

Mail Order and Home Delivery Suppliers

Something that has grown enormously in the past decade is the invaluable facility to do at least some of the Christmas shopping in the comfort of your own home by the means of mail order. It avoids the crowds, queues and hassle, and although you have to take into account postal and delivery charges these can be offset against transport and parking costs, which are becoming more and more exorbitant.

If you are a lover of really good food, may I first point you in the direction of an award-winning book called *British Food Finds* by Henrietta Green, which lists by region and product a large number of local food producers. The book is updated each year and is available by post from Book for Cooks (4 Blenheim Crescent, London W11 1NN Tel: 071 221 1992). You will be amazed in fact at how many producers of fine foods there are in your own area, and some of them offer postal and delivery services. Below I have set out some names and addresses of suppliers that are personally recommended – but do make sure you phone first for a catalogue and details of current prices.

Suffolk Cured Hams
Emmetts, Peasenhall, Suffolk
072879 250

York Hams and Bradenham Hams
Harris-Leeming Bar, Leases Road,
Leeming Bar, Northallerton
North Yorkshire DL7 9AW   0677 422661

Venison
Reediehill Deer Farm, Reediehill,
Fife KY14 7HS

Geese
Judy Goodman, Goodman's Geese,
Walsgrove Farm, Great Witley,
Worcs. WR6 6JJ   0299 896272

Homemade Produce (jams, pickles,
chutney, preserves, homemade pies, cakes,
Christmas puddings, hampers)
Suffolk Larder Foods,
17 The Thoroughfare, Woodbridge,
Suffolk IP12 1AA   0394 386676

Turkeys (bronze, black and white)
Derek Kelly Turkeys Ltd, Springate Farm,
Danbury, Essex CM3 4EP   0245 223581
Munson, Emdon Straight Road, Boxted,
Colchester CO4 5QX   0206 272637

Scottish Smoked Salmon
Dunkeld Smoked Salmon,
Springwells Smokehouse, Brae Street,
Dunkeld, Perthshire PH8 0BA   0350 727639

Fine Chocolates
Charbonnel et Walker, 1 The Royal Arcade,
28 Old Bond Street, London W1X 4BT
071 491 0939 (24 hours)

Freshly Roasted Coffee & Fine Teas
H. R. Higgins (Coffeeman) Ltd,
79 Duke Street, London W1M 6AS
071 629 3913/071 491 8819

Cake Decorating (including holly leaf cutters)
Twitters, 81 Hoe Street, Walthamstow,
London E17 4SA   081 520 0525

Kitchen Equipment
All equipment mentioned in this book should be available at good kitchen shops everywhere. But, if you have difficulty obtaining things like the lattice cutter or the small metal pudding basins, postal services are provided by Divertimenti, 139–141 Fulham Road, London SW3   071 581 8065 and Lakeland Plastics Ltd, Alexandra Buildings, Windermere, Cumbria LA23 1BQ   05394 88100

TURKEY SIZES AND TIMINGS

A good size of turkey for the average family is 12–14 lb (about 5.5–6.5 kg). This is oven-ready weight – which is equivalent to 14–16 lb (6.5–7.5 kg) New York dressed weight. But below you'll find cooking times for varying sizes of turkey.

It might be helpful to beginners if I give you an account of the exact timings of a recent turkey of mine. The turkey (14 lb/6.5 kg oven-ready weight) went into the oven, pre-heated to gas mark 7, 425°F (220°C), at 8.15 am. The heat was lowered to gas mark 3, 325°F (170°C), at 8.55. The foil came off and the heat was turned up to gas mark 6, 400°F (200°C), at 12.30. Then, with lots of basting, it was cooked by 1.15 and served by 2.00.

Cooking times for other sizes of turkey

8–10 lb turkey (3.5–4.5 kg):
30 minutes at the high temperature, then 2½–3 hours at the lower temperature, then a final 30 minutes (uncovered) at gas mark 6, 400°F (200°C).

15–20 lb turkey (6.75–9 kg):
45 minutes at the high temperature, then 4–5 hours at the lower temperature, then a final 30 minutes (uncovered) at gas mark 6, 400°F (200°C).

Please bear in mind that ovens, and turkeys themselves, vary and the only sure way of knowing if a bird is ready is by using the tests described in the recipe.

FROZEN TURKEYS

Try if possible to get a fresh bird. However, if you can only buy a frozen bird, or it's more convenient to do so, try to buy one that has been frozen without added water, then don't forget to allow plenty of time for it to de-frost slowly and *completely*. Always remove the giblets as soon as you can – with a fresh bird immediately you get home, with a frozen one as soon as it has thawed.

Index

•

Conversion Tables

Aᴸᴸ these are approximate conversions, which have either been rounded up or down. In a few recipes it has been necessary to modify them very slightly. Never mix metric and imperial measures in one recipe, stick to one system or the other. All spoon measurements used throughout this book are level unless specified otherwise.

OVEN TEMPERATURES

Mark 1	275°F	140°C
2	300	150
3	325	170
4	350	180
5	375	190
6	400	200
7	425	220
8	450	230
9	475	240

MEASUREMENTS

⅛ inch	3 mm
¼	5 mm
½	1 cm
¾	2
1	2.5
1¼	3
1½	4
1¾	4.5
2	5
2½	6
3	7.5
3½	9
4	10
5	13
5¼	13.5
6	15
6½	16
7	18
7½	19
8	20
9	23
9½	24
10	25.5
11	28
12	30

WEIGHTS

½ oz	10 g
¾	20
1	25
1½	40
2	50
2½	60
3	75
4	110
4½	125
5	150
6	175
7	200
8	225
9	250
10	275
12	350
1 lb	450
1½	700
2	900
3	1.35 kg

VOLUME

2 fl oz	55 ml
3	75
5 (¼ pt)	150
½ pt	275
¾	425
1	570
1¼	725
1¾	1 litre
2	1.2
2½	1.5
4	2.25